FORESIGHT
IS 20/20

FORESIGHT
IS 20/20

Unlock
Your Past to
Create a
Better future

Nathan Lancry

To the certain few who believed in me, even though at the time they couldn't see.

Contents

Introduction

The Motorcycle That Wasn't What He Thought It Was

During March of 1998, a high-end motorcycle dealer approached a wealthy Kentucky car collector named Cole Rodriguez with a tantalizing offer. The mysterious bike seller claimed he had the winning motorcycle from Daytona three years earlier—a bike built by legendary New Zealand mechanic John Britten. There are just ten John Britten V1000s in existence, and this is the only one to win at Daytona. The body is an elegant frosted blue and it has an almost cartoonish appearance. It is exceptionally rare. The dealer wanted $250,000 for it.

For Rodriguez, a highly skilled and successful car collector, this was the perfect opportunity to start his motorcycle collection—something he'd been dying to do for years. Rodriguez hired Niall Stromm, an automotive expert, to review the bike. It had the classic Britten build, Stromm confirmed, with a wide front fairing seated above an extra narrow engine assembly, like a torpedo atop a knife blade. Stromm also confirmed the dealer had mountains of paperwork certifying the bike's authenticity. John Britten had owned the machine himself in 1995 when he died from an aggressive form of cancer. Then the bike disappeared from the public eye for a few years before resurfacing recently in the possession of Britten's cousin.

A chemist from the University of Pittsburgh, Susan Rothmire, spent four days taking the bike apart and probing the pieces with a transmission electron microscope. She removed a .5cm sample of material from beneath the gas cap and analyzed it using optical emission spectroscopy, neutron activation analysis, X-ray fluorescence, and Schöniger oxidation. The outer body was made of hand-formed carbon fiber with traces of halloysite clay inside. This was important because halloysite comes from Matauri Bay in New Zealand, nearby where Britten did his work. And Britten famously shaped his bikes on a chicken wire frame covered in clay.

It seemed the bike was authentic.

Satisfied with his investigation after weeks of intense research, Rodriguez agreed to purchase the motorcycle. He threw an unveiling party and invited the press. Motorcycle World magazine did a front page spread. So did Bike Collector, Speed Watch, and many others. Rodriguez was praised as a visionary collector who was making an exceptional first foray into motorcycles. At the party, people waited in line for over an hour to take a photo of themselves sitting on the bike.

However, something about the motorcycle wasn't right. The first person to notice it was Al Lambert, a mechanic and motorcycle enthusiast who had studied the work of John Britten closely. "Cole took me to look at the bike," Al remembers, "and he flipped on the lights and I said I hope you can get your money back." What did Al notice? He couldn't say. He just had a gut feeling something was wrong. Mary Warsaw voiced a similar sentiment. She's a journalist who has written extensively about Britten and his work. When she saw photos of the bike that her magazine was planning to publish she called her editor. "I told him the bike is fake," she recalls. "I asked if it was too late to pull the story."

With all the red flags, Rodriguez got worried. He brought the V1000 to the next motorcycle show to have more experts look at it. There, the negative impressions continued.

One man, an engineer for Ducati, grimaced when he laid eyes on the bike. Another, a motorcycle historian, shook his head. Then there was the European collector who gasped in horror when Rodriguez showed him the V1000. By the time the show was over, everyone was talking about the Britten bike. Many felt something about it was wrong. Rodriguez had come to one conclusion with his chemical analysis and review of the paperwork, but some of the top motorcycle experts in the world disagreed based on a gut feeling.

For some time it wasn't clear who was right. But then, one piece at a time, the case Rodriguez had assembled began to fall apart. The paperwork linking the bike to Britten's cousin, for instance, was forged. One invoice, dated 1995, refers to a bank account that didn't exist until 1997. A letter from 1994 includes a phone number that was cancelled in 1993. Originally, Rodriguez had determined the bike to be in John Britten's later style, but the experts pointed out flaws with that conclusion too. The bike did feature Britten's famous skin-and-bones chassis, with slender carbon fiber segments winding delicately around the engine cylinders, but it's front telescopic fork didn't include the double wishbone suspension system Britten adopted later in his career. The bike that most closely resembled Rodriguez's was a toy created by the Guggenheim museum for their gift shop to accompany their Art of the Motorcycle exhibit. And what about the scientific analysis proving the motorcycle body was made near Britten's home? The results rested on traces of New Zealand clay that were found inside the body. But halloysite clay, it turns out, can be ordered anywhere in the world for a small shipping fee. And it was common knowledge Britten used it to shape the bodies of his bikes.

Rodriguez never tried to sell the motorcycle, and he stopped listing it as part of his collection.

What made this Kentucky car collector so confident he could buy a quarter-million dollar motorcycle when he knew almost nothing about bikes? Why did his careful analysis lead him in exactly the wrong direction?

Cole Rodriguez had a lapse in foresight—and it cost him $250,000.

The exact same psychological biases that caused Rodriguez to make the wrong decision about that motorcycle affect all of us. We all lack foresight in some areas of our lives. This explains why you can't seem to get the body you want, even though you eat healthy and exercise regularly. It reveals why you don't have the level of professional success you desire, even though you're intelligent and hardworking. It can also show why you don't have the kind of romantic and social relationships you deserve and crave, even though you're caring, friendly, and physically attractive.

This book is about the science of becoming more self aware—why we are sometimes caught off guard and what we can all do to have 20/20 vision before we get involved in anything. Hindsight is always 20/20, but it's time we appreciate how foresight can be 20/20 as well. I'm not talking about seeing the future. I'm talking about seeing the present so clearly you can anticipate the future. To get there you'll have to unlock your past.

What You Don't Know Can Hurt You

Stare straight ahead without moving your eyes. Now, how much of the room can you see clearly? Are you able to make out 80% of your surroundings? Or maybe 60%? Take a moment to try it out for yourself and decide on a number.

After posing this scenario to thousands of people over the years, I've found the typical response to be 60-70%. Nearly everyone believes they can see at least 50% of the room clearly. But this is far from the truth.

The key word in those last two paragraphs is *clearly*. The human eye has a high concentration of sensors in the center of the retina, known as the fovea centralis. That's the scientific term for the small area in the center of your eye where you can see everything with extreme clarity. And it only makes up about 1% of our field of vision. That's right, 1%! To illustrate this, let's do a small experiment. Stare at the **X** below. Then, without moving your eyes, try to read the following paragraph using only your peripheral vision.

X

Can you do it? Are you reading this whole paragraph without moving your eyes from the **X**? This task, it turns out, is impossible. The human eye simply does not perceive much detail except for in the very center. We feel like we can see the whole room clearly but this is, in fact, an illusion. Your brain is playing tricks on you. Your eyes are seeing fuzzy shapes and your mind is filling in the rest. In fact, your extreme peripheral vision functions almost exclusively in black and white. Even the colors are filled in by your brain.

But yet, most of us are confident our peripheral vision is clear.

Even within the 1% of your visual field that you can see clearly, your perception is further limited by what you choose to focus on. In a famous study by Daniel Simmons and Christopher Chabris, people were asked to watch a video featuring two teams of basketball players each passing a different basketball. The researchers instructed their subjects to count how many times the white team passed the ball.

After watching the video, almost every subject correctly answered that the white team passed the ball 15 times. The researchers then asked the subjects a surprising question: "Did you see the gorilla?" When half of the subjects said no, the researchers rewound the tape. Sure enough, right in the middle of the video, a person in a gorilla costume walks into the middle of the scene, beats its chest, and walks off screen. This phenomenon of selective attention has since been nicknamed *The Invisible Gorilla* effect.

Even when valuable information is right in the center of our vision, we can miss it if our attention is focused elsewhere.

"A lot of what we see and conclude about the world is authored by our brains," says David Dunning, a psychologist at the University of Michigan who has spent his career studying this phenomenon. This isn't just true about our visual field, Dunning explains, it's a universal human bias. "Whenever we reach a conclusion, it just seems like it's the right one."

In other words, when we have a little bit of information about something, we easily convince ourselves we can see the whole picture. We do this in virtually every area of our lives, says Dunning. "Even though your belief about the way the world is just seems so compelling or self-evident, it doesn't mean it really is [true]."

Dunning's work on this subject, along with his colleague, Justin Kruger, was so influential the phenomenon has been nicknamed the Dunning-Kruger Effect. In their 1999 paper titled *Unskilled and Unaware of It*, Dunning and Kruger administered a series of tests to college students at Cornell University. Before revealing their scores, the researchers asked the participants to estimate how well they did. Regardless of whether the test covered grammar, logical reasoning, or humor, the results were nearly identical: the lowest scoring students felt they did fairly well. Participants scoring in the 10th percentile (they did worse than 90% of their peers) rated their abilities in the 67th percentile. These students had terrible grammar, flawed logic, and a horrible sense of humor, but they thought they were in the top third of all people.

And it's not just students who display this tendency to overestimate our abilities. A national survey of Americans revealed that 21% believe they are 'very likely' or 'fairly likely' to become millionaires within the next ten years. A study at the University of Nebraska found that 90% of teachers think they are above average. A survey of several hundred engineers revealed that 32% at one company and 42% at another rated themselves as performing among the top 5% of their peers. In a study of common clinical procedures among medical interns, 80% asserted they understood bladder catheterization well enough to teach it to someone else. However, trained tutors disagreed. Half of the interns were rated as not competent enough to perform the procedure without supervision and *none* were deemed competent enough to teach it.

It doesn't matter how motivated people are to accurately assess their abilities, we still tend to overestimate our skills. In one study, researchers offered participants a $100 reward if they could guess how they performed on a test. However, this incentive did not make people any more accurate at judging their own knowledge.

For Cole Rodriguez the fact that he had $250,000 on the line when he bought the Britten V1000 didn't make a difference, he still fell hard for the Dunning-Kruger Effect. In fact, there were several factors at play that made Rodriguez overestimate his ability to buy a motorcycle. When these factors exist, we are all more likely to lack foresight.

First, though he knew little about motorcycles, Rodriguez was already a successful collector of automobiles. Studies have shown that people with genuine expertise in one domain are more likely to mistakenly believe those skills and knowledge can be applied to related areas where they have less experience. For instance, in one study, Dunning asked participants to rate how familiar they were with various terms related to topics like science, politics, and geography. Some of the terms were real while others were made up. Interestingly, participants who claimed to be more knowledgeable about the topic were also more likely to falsely assert they understood the nonsense words. When you're knowledgeable in one area, you tend to feel overly confident in related areas too.

Second, Rodriguez was also prone to a lapse in foresight because he did some research on the bike but stopped short of consulting a true John Britten expert. In a series of six studies, Dunning has found strong evidence for a 'beginner's bubble' of confidence. When we are exposed to a small amount of information or gain a small amount of experience in a certain domain, we are particularly likely to overestimate our abilities. For instance, when participants were first asked to calculate 45 + 56 they became more confident they could correctly perform the calculation 45 x 56, even though the addition problem made them no more likely to get the multiplication right. The fact that the participants had a sense of familiarity with the problem gave them the feeling they were more capable than they truly were.

Even just a little bit of exposure to a subject can create the illusion that you know more about it than you really do. Thus, experiences from our past prevent us from holding a clear vision of the future.

In the case of Cole Rodriguez, he was overconfident in his ability to purchase a $250,000 motorcycle because he knew a lot about cars, which are very similar to motorcycles, and he did some research on the bike—so he knew a little about it. However, it turns out he did the wrong kind of research. He hired a general automotive expert and a chemist. But he didn't seek out someone who was an expert on John Britten's work. As soon as Al Lambert and Mary Warsaw laid eyes on the motorcycle they knew something was wrong with it. These people were true John Britten experts, so they could see the problems right away.

Had he consulted them before he signed the check to buy the bike, Rodriguez might have saved himself from making a colossal error.

And the same is true for all of us every day of our lives. We all experience lapses in foresight constantly. But we can learn to see more clearly. And it starts by getting clear about the past.

Hindsight is 20/20...But not Foresight

Do you know how a helicopter works? I'm not talking about the wiring schematics, air pressure gauges, navigation systems, and engine—I just mean the basics of how a helicopter lifts off and flies through the air. Could you sketch a simple diagram and explain it to a friend? How confident are you in your knowledge on a scale of 1 to 10?

In a 2002 study conducted at Yale University, most participants were certain they at least knew the basics of helicopter flight. But then the researchers asked for an explanation of one of the most fundamental aspects of helicopter aviation: how, exactly, does a helicopter transition from hovering in the air to moving forward? When the pilot pushes forward on the joystick, what causes the aircraft to tip forward and begin to accelerate?

Most of the participants were stumped and the exercise caused them to rethink their initial estimates of how well they understood helicopters. They realized they'd been fooling themselves into thinking they understood these machines better than they really did.

How did you perform on this? Take a second and record a quick voice memo of yourself explaining the mechanics of helicopter acceleration and then go check your response online. Were you anywhere near the truth? Did this exercise cause you to lower your initial assessment of your knowledge?

Maybe that's an unfair example. After all, most of us have only ridden in a helicopter once or twice, if at all. Let's take a device everyone is more familiar with: a bicycle. Before you read further, rate yourself again on a scale of 1 to 10 when it comes to your knowledge of the basic workings of a bike. Do you know what makes it move forward? How do the brakes function?

In a 2006 study published in *Memory & Cognition*, psychologist Rebecca Lawson asked participants to draw a basic diagram of a bicycle and found that many people, and women in particular, were unable to correctly position the chain and pedals. Even some expert bike mechanics made simple errors in their diagrams. After struggling to draw a sketch, most participants ultimately concluded they didn't understand bicycles as well as they initially thought.

Using the diagram below, give it a shot for yourself. Use a pen to fill in the missing portions of the frame and add pedals and a chain where you think they belong.

How did you do? In Lawson's study, over 40% of the participants made errors in their drawings and most realized after attempting the sketch that they didn't understand the mechanics of a bicycle nearly as well as they'd anticipated. Even when Lawson merely asked people to select the proper chain and pedal configuration from a series of options, many couldn't do it.

Here are a few samples of the types of errors people commonly made during the study.

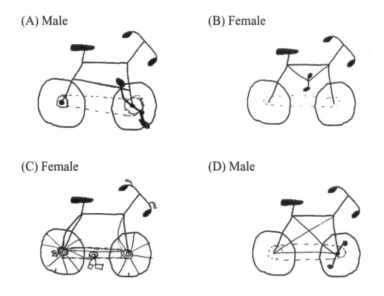

The same exact effect has been demonstrated by asking people how well they understand a litany of other common household items, like a zipper, piano key, flush toilet, sewing machine, and speedometer. Time and again results reveal that most people feel they understand the world around them with much greater ease, clarity, and richness than is actually the case. We think we know how things work, but we don't really.

Psychologists refer to this phenomenon as the Illusion of Explanatory Depth, and it has been demonstrated in dozens of situations.

So, why am I talking about motorcycles, helicopters, and bikes in a book about how to have more foresight? Who cares if you don't completely understand the inner workings of your refrigerator, toaster oven, and coffee maker, as long as you can use them to chill your beer, heat up your leftovers, and brew your morning java?

The problem isn't that we don't understand how things function. That's unavoidable in today's complex world. Nobody understands how everything works. Rather, the issue is that we are *overconfident* in our ability to explain things. We don't understand, but we convince ourselves that we do.

At its core, the act of assessing our own competence involves predicting the future. When I asked you how well you could explain the workings of a helicopter you had to imagine yourself trying to teach someone how the machine works and then evaluate the quality of your response. The Dunning-Kruger Effect, along with the Illusion of Explanatory Depth, are examples of lapses in foresight. We are terrible, it turns out, at predicting how well we will perform on a certain task.

Imagine yourself sitting in the cockpit of a helicopter at this moment. Would you risk your life attempting to fly that helicopter? If the answer is no (which I hope it is), why would you take similar risks with your emotional state by making decisions about things you're not an expert in, like Cole Rodriguez did with the bike?

The future is a wonderful place. We all tend to imagine that one day soon we are going to ace the test, get the job, quit smoking, work up the nerve to tell our boss where to shove it, learn how to tango dance, raise amazing kids, and retire early to a life of relaxation, tranquility, abundance, happiness, and inner peace. Cole Rodriguez had succeeded with cars in the past, so he easily imagined a future in which he was a brilliant and savvy motorcycle collector. He was confident enough in this delusional view of his potential to fork out $250,000 dollars for his first bike.

Hindsight may be 20/20 but foresight is anything but. When it comes to predicting the future, we are all wildly delusional. And the problem is our past experiences.

Studies show this phenomenon exists across the board. We are madly over-confident in our ability to predict the outcome of a sporting match, forecast what will happen in the economy, estimate what we'll be doing in a year, or determine whether we'll be able to repeat a certain action again a few minutes later. We look backward and tell ourselves we would have guessed the last outcome. Then we look forward and assume we can confidently guess the next one. But we are wrong.

It's easy to think this must be something *other* people suffer from. But you and I, of course, are immune. Lapses in foresight must be really common among certain people. But not me, right?

How often do you see someone suffering the consequences of a poor decision or circumstance on the news and think, "That will never happen to me." But what evidence do you have that supports this belief? The truth is that anything can happen to you. So where does this grandiose mindset come from?

In one clever set of studies conducted by Richard West and Keith Stanovich, the researchers selected two tasks that were as different as possible: a knowledge assessment and a motor performance test. Were the people who displayed the biggest lapses in foresight in regard to their mental abilities the same ones who failed to accurately predict their physical skills? Nope. There was no significant association between the two.

We all have some areas of life where we are true experts. In these domains, we may demonstrate a high degree of foresight. However, we also all have many blind spots. The location of these blind spots is different for all of us but the universal truth is that we aren't aware they exist. Just as your brain fills in your peripheral vision and makes you feel like you can see the whole room in perfect clarity, so too does it fill in your gaps in foresight.

You don't know what you don't know, that's the problem—or should I say that's the *opportunity*. The things you feel most confident and self assured about might be the very places where you are most vulnerable to making colossal errors in judgment. Think about the 90% of teachers who believe they are well above average in their abilities. Or the 21% of Americans who are convinced they'll be millionaires in less than 10 years. Or the 32-42% of engineers who are certain they are among the top 5% of performers at their organization.

At times, we all live in a fantasy world, fueled by a grandiose mindset. Because this error is so common, learning how to overcome it will put you miles ahead of what you've previously imagined for your future growth.

If you want to achieve better results in your life, you must understand where these lapses in foresight come from, how to spot them, and what you can do to manage them. You must realize where you have been lying to yourself and be willing to face the truth. Give yourself permission to make mistakes and don't be hard on yourself for the learning curve. It's not easy, but the results are more than worth it. Implement the tools in this book and you will be able to achieve the life you've always wanted. First we have to shatter your illusions and break you out of your grandiose mindset.

Hindsight is 20/20, and foresight is usually not—but foresight is your area of opportunity. By implementing the strategies in this book, you will examine your past to become more aware of your blindspots. Then you'll leverage foresight to create any life you want.

Just don't go rushing to buy any expensive motorcycles…

Chapter 1
The Track of Humility

Roger Peterson wrestled with the controls and squinted through the front window of the airplane, trying desperately to make out the horizon and get his bearings through the gathering storm. Low clouds and light snowfall obscured his view, and the area was sparsely populated, meaning there were no lights on the ground he could use for reference. He looked down at the instrument panel, his heart hammering in his chest.

Nine months earlier Peterson had failed an instrument checkride, so he wasn't certified to operate the plane in weather conditions that required use of the instruments. He'd logged just 52 hours of instrument training in his short career as a pilot, and all of that training had been on airplanes equipped with a conventional artificial horizon as a source of aircraft altitude information. This plane, however, had an older Sperry F3 gyroscope, which displays the pitch and altitude information in the opposite direction.

His knuckles were white on the joystick and his palms dripped with sweat as he struggled to make sense of the lights and dials on the dashboard. He took a deep breath to calm his nerves but fear gripped him so strongly that he felt paralyzed. His brain wasn't working properly.

This plane wasn't a cargo flight, like Peterson was used to flying. In fact, the passengers huddled in the cabin behind him were Buddy Holly, Ritchie Valens, and "The Big Bopper" J. P. Richardson—three of the biggest musicians in the world.

Peterson cursed himself for agreeing to this flight at the last minute. The weather briefing he'd been given before boarding the plane hadn't mentioned any kind of adverse flying conditions. His boss, Jerry Dwyer, normally would have taken such a difficult and important flight, but he'd been unavailable because of a prior commitment, so Roger Peterson got the call.

The series of events that led Peterson to be sitting in that cockpit didn't begin that night, the problems started three weeks earlier. These passengers never would have needed to charter that flight in the first place if their touring company had more foresight.

The perilous situation was completely avoidable.

The tour began when superstar Buddy Holly decided to join the Winter Dance Party tour with General Artist Corporation. He'd signed an unfavorable contract with his previous record company, so the executives were earning the bulk of the royalties on his bestselling hits while he was starving. And with his firstborn child on the way, Holly was in a pinch for some extra money.

The Winter Dance Party tour was scheduled to play in twenty-four Midwestern cities in twenty-four days. General Artists prioritized a full schedule and ignored geography. It didn't matter if Tuesday's show was two states over from Wednesday's show, and Thursday's was somewhere in between. If the band had to zigzag across the country, exceeding 400 miles and 12 hours on the road each day, so be it. Off days meant no money would be made, and that was unacceptable to the record executives.

The tour organizers didn't hire roadies or assistants either. To save money, they left the musicians to unload, set up, and sound check their own equipment, put on a hell of a rock concert, reload their gear the same night, and hit the road to get to the next town by morning. In 1959, the Interstate Highway System had not been fully developed, so the journeys between concerts were long and treacherous. The "highways" were unlit, rural two-lane roads strewn with potholes and snow drifts that challenged the bands' vehicles—and their sanity.

The tour bus wasn't equipped to handle deep snow and subzero temperatures. The engine worked overtime to push through the unwieldy roads for hundreds of miles at a time. Eventually it gave out. In the first eleven days of the tour, the bus was replaced four times. One replacement didn't have a heating system. Desperate to stay on schedule, the band agreed to use the bus, despite outside temperatures of -20°F.

Then the engine failed on Highway 51 in the middle of the night.

Bandmate Tommy Allsup recalls that his skin went cold with fear when the lights of the tour bus began to dim. As they drove up a steep incline, battling intense snowfall, the bus started to moan and creek. Then it ground to a stop.

"The bus is frozen," murmured the driver.

It was pitch black and they were sitting in the road, in the middle of nowhere, without lights or heat. Everyone on board worried they might freeze to death.

The musicians lit bonfires from crumpled up newspapers and huddled under blankets. The drummer, Carl Bunch, suffered hypothermia as he struggled to move. Allsup's feet turned black.

It wasn't until sunrise that headlights finally appeared on the horizon. It was the sheriff's deputy. A passing trucker had noticed the marooned bus and alerted the authorities. The sheriff brought the musicians to Hurley, Wisconsin, while Bunch was taken to a nearby hospital.

Monday, Feb. 2 was supposed to be an off-day to recuperate in Hurley. Thankfully, the night's show had been postponed due to tempestuous weather. But at the last minute, tour organizers booked a "make-up" show in a town called Clear Lake, Iowa, some 350 miles away. So the tired musicians piled back onto the bus and headed north.

At the Clear Lake show, Holly's frustration with the "Tour from Hell" reached a boiling point. He couldn't take it anymore. He was delirious, overworked, and desperate. Meanwhile, his bandmates were growing increasingly ill and frostbitten. Their next show was 400 miles from Clear Lake in Moorhead, Minnesota.

There was no way Buddy Holly was getting back on that bus. He called Valens and Richardson into a private dressing room and said "I've chartered a plane, we're the guys making the money. We should be the ones flying ahead."

According to one of Holly's tourmates, Dion, he had originally planned to take his remaining Crickets, Allsup and Jennings, on the plane. However, they decided to give up their seats to Valens and Richardson. Allsup lost out to Valens in a last-minute coin toss. Jennings's seat went to the Big Bopper because he was sick with the flu.

When Buddy learned his bass player had lost his seat to Richarson, he smirked and said "Well, I hope your damned bus freezes up again."

"Well, I hope your plane crashes," snapped Jennings.

Those words would haunt him for years.

Shortly after takeoff, the inexperienced pilot lost control and crashed into a nearby field. In the morning, four bodies were identified: Holly, Valens, Richardson, and the pilot, Roger Peterson. This crash has become known as The Day the Music Died, and it's immortalized in the hit song American Pie by Don McLean.

Who was to blame for this tragedy? Was it the pilot's fault for agreeing to the flight in the first place? Or was it the shortsighted decisions of a desperate band member? Or the touring company that brewed up the perfect storm for disaster?

A closer inspection reveals the flying service, the musicians, and the tour managers were all on a collision course with doom and no one stopped to think about it. If just one of the three parties had better foresight, this tragic incident could have been avoided.

Powerful foresight comes from having the right people in our corner. We all have blind spots, but we can't see them for ourselves. We need people who will show us what we are overlooking and what we lack. We need a panel of personal advisors with the right motivations and credentials to help us see what we can't see.

Without a panel of the right kind of people, we will be swept into impulsive decisions and our blind spots will grow larger.

As we navigate any challenge there is a narrow path we must stay on to ensure we achieve the result we want. I call it the Track of Humility. However, along the way to the outcome you desire there are three checkpoints you must get past. At each checkpoint there are strong forces that seek to pull you off the Track of Humility. Without the right people in your corner to point out your blind spots, it's virtually impossible to make it through all three checkpoints successfully and reach your goal.

At the first checkpoint the forces will threaten to pull you into the trap of setting unrealistic expectations. At the second checkpoint you'll be tempted to adopt entitled thinking and ignore warning signs. Finally, at the third checkpoint, the forces will push you to convince yourself you're someone you aren't. It might sound easy to set the right expectations, avoid entitled thinking, and be honest with ourselves, but the reality is we're quite bad at it. Studies show that people consistently fall off the Track of Humility in these three key areas as we strive to pursue a goal.

To overcome these checkpoints and develop deeper foresight, we have to get the right people in our corner. But before we can learn how to do that, we need to talk about the checkpoints in more depth. How do they work? What makes them so difficult to avoid?

Checkpoint 1: Know Where You're At To Know Where You're Going

Imagine you are in the passenger seat of a car, blindfolded. You can hear the sound of other cars passing on the highway. You feel the car accelerate up an incline, and then slow down as it turns onto a gravelly road. You can hear the crunch of gravel and feel the vibrations through the wheels beneath you. Then the car stops. The blindfold is removed, and you can see that you are in a forest on a mountain. The mysterious driver gives you an old map, a flashlight, a water bottle, and a day's worth of food.

The driver then says you are allowed to ask one question, and one question only, before you are left alone on the mountain. What question do you ask?

There is only one question to ask: "Where am I on this map?"

Once you know where you are then you can figure out where you want to go, and how to get there. Until you know your emotional and geographical location, everything else is irrelevant.

The first checkpoint on the journey of humility is the challenge of setting realistic expectations. When we opt for mental shortcuts that lead us to over-estimate or underestimate our anticipated outcomes, we can find ourselves in undesirable situations. We set unrealistic expectations because although our brains are incredibly powerful, they're a bit lazy. It might be difficult to imagine how one of the most complex wonders of machinery on earth—an organ with the ability to create consciousness, design mile-high skyscrapers, and consider paradoxes that would burn out the most high-end computers—could possibly be thought of as lazy. But studies show it's true.

Comprising only about 2% of our total body weight, the brain consumes 20% of our oxygen and a quarter of our energy over the course of the day. When we're low on blood sugar, tired, or in a rush, our brain takes shortcuts to accomplish its myriad tasks all at once. These shortcuts can be lifesaving when you're in real danger, but when we use them repeatedly we lose our ability to compose realistic expectations.

Do you ever watch scary movies with friends just for the rush of adrenaline? Some of us love the thrill of being scared in a recreational environment. Others tend to get dragged along, finding ourselves squirming at the grotesque images on the screen. When an alien's tentacle shoots out of the darkness and grabs at the camera like a chameleon's tongue, you might jump in your seat. Your automatic (lazy) brain perceives danger, so you scream and flinch to pro-tect your vital organs. A more thoughtful brain might say, "pixels on the screen cannot really hurt me," but your lazy brain prepares you for the worst anyway, allowing your friend to chuckle with enjoyment as you shield your face with your hands.

Don't let such a friend get under your skin, though, because your brain has good reason to be reacting to the scary movie. If the two of you were to go on a hike and suddenly encounter a fang-flaring snake blocking your path, the friend who has numbed his automatic response to fearful stimuli might find fang holes in his buttocks while you're already halfway up a tree.

Mental shortcuts can protect us from harm, but they can also skew our expectations. Take the following math problem for example:

$1 \times 2 \times 3 \times 4 \times 5 \times 6 \times 7 \times 8 = ?$

Without using a calculator or even doing longhand multiplication on a piece of paper, take a guess at the answer to this problem. Don't overthink this, just consider the numbers and use your best judgment to estimate the answer. Once you have a number in your mind, do the same for the following problem as well:

$8 \times 7 \times 6 \times 5 \times 4 \times 3 \times 2 \times 1 = ?$

The astute reader may have realized these are the exact same math problem. The numbers have simply been rearranged. However, when students are given one of these expressions and told to solve it on the spot without a calculator, they produce wildly different answers depending on the order of the numbers. The average answer for one of the math problems is 512, while the other is 2,250. Can you guess which is which?

$1 \times 2 \times 3 \times 4 \times 5 \times 6 \times 7 \times 8 \approx 512$
$8 \times 7 \times 6 \times 5 \times 4 \times 3 \times 2 \times 1 \approx 2,250$

How can we possibly be this bad at estimating the solution to a simple math problem? Why do our expectations about the answer get thrown off by merely rearranging the numbers? We get caught at the first checkpoint. The reason is because this problem is very difficult to compute without a calculator. Thus, we end up using a mental shortcut. In our heads, we multiply the first few numbers in the sequence. Then we get lazy and estimate the rest of the problem based on that initial number. Multiplying lower numbers first yields a lower product, so we expect the overall answer to be low. On the other hand, starting with the bigger numbers creates a much larger initial product, so we expect the product to be larger.

Our expectations are strongly influenced by the first thing that pops into our heads. That's how we are able to look at the same basic problem and arrive at different estimates of the answer. If you were to pull out a calculator right now to see which estimate is closer, you might be shocked. The true value of this equation is 40,320. Both guesses are way off.

This failure to set appropriate expectations is due to a psychological bias called anchoring. We assign too much weight to initial information, skewing our judgment. When new information is presented, we struggle to adjust our expectations accordingly. Anchoring is one of the forces that pulls us off the Track of Humility at the first checkpoint.

Another force that often pulls us into unrealistic expectations is something you might have noticed at play with cupcakes in the breakroom. When it's someone's birthday at the office you might celebrate by leaving out a box of delicious frosted cupcakes. If there are a dozen cupcakes for your office of sixteen people, some colleagues will have to skip dessert. However, if the cupcakes were cut in half, you're guaranteed to have leftovers.

This well-documented behavior operates on a mental shortcut called the unit bias. Each person will consume one dessert unit on average, regardless of how big or small the units are. With a slice of the knife, twelve dessert units become twenty-four dessert units. The brain sees no difference between a halved cupcake and a whole cupcake when it craves dessert. The sweet-toothed coworker who eats two half cupcakes also would have eaten two whole cupcakes if they weren't cut in half.

Researchers find that portion size directly correlates with calorie consumption due to the unit bias. Whether the serving size is 100g, 150g, or 200g, the brain expects it to be one universal unit. We'll eat more if our serving size is bigger and not notice. Is it rational? Absolutely not. Do we do it anyway? Yep.

Another example of how our expectations can get seriously warped at the first checkpoint comes from the research on labels. Grocery stores and marketers have discovered that putting organic or vegan labels on products makes them more attractive to consumers. In one study, participants were asked to rate three pairs of products: two yogurts, two cookies and two servings of potato chips. One was labeled 'organic,' while the other was labeled 'regular.' Organic yogurt was perceived as being far lower in fat and much more appetizing. Organic chips were estimated to have fewer calories, and to taste better.

Even after sampling each pair of products (which were completely identical), the participants still held inaccurate expectations about their calorie content and healthiness. Just like the math problem we saw earlier, participants based their expectations on their initial inputs. Because they expected healthy, organic desserts wouldn't be as delicious, they rated them as tasting much worse than the regular ones.

The same effect applies to wine. We expect expensive wine to taste better than cheap wine. When the exact same wine is poured into two different bottles, the one with the cheap price tag gets a lower rating than the one with the pricey label. One study even allowed participants to sample different wines through a straw while seated in a brain scanner. The reward centers of the brain lit up more when the wine was supposedly higher priced. Our false expectations shape how we taste products and interact with the world.

We're so bad at creating realistic expectations that many of us develop aviophobia, the fear of flying, because we worry our plane might crash. According to a Norweigan study, over 20 million Americans have clinical-level anxiety around flying. It's understandable if you think soaring in a metal tube at 30,000 feet in the air sounds a bit risky, but plane accidents are far less prevalent than car accidents. Chances are, you're significantly more likely to crash on the way to the airport than you are in the airplane itself. Unfortunately, this reassuring piece of data isn't the first thing that comes to most Americans' minds when they think of airplane safety.

After the terrorist attacks on September 11, 2001, Americans were less likely to travel by plane and prefered to go by car. People expected air travel would be risky because they were shaken up about the tragedy at the World Trade Center. As a result, fatalities from auto accidents spiked in the weeks following 9/11. Car crashes kill about 40,000 people in America each year, while airplane crashes kill less than 1000 people worldwide.

The reason we have unrealistic expectations about air travel is because airplane crashes are so horrifying they receive significant news coverage when they do occur, whereas auto accidents are so common and mundane they rarely make the front page of the paper. For this reason, we expect airplanes to crash more often than they actually do.

Just like the participants trying to estimate the solution to the multiplication problem a few pages back, we are terrible at estimating the chances of our airplane crashing. Our expectations are completely off base, and it can cause us to make foolish decisions, like driving long distances instead of flying.

Even seasoned experts, it turns out, are terrible at setting accurate expectations of future performance and are often pulled off the Track of Humility at the first checkpoint.

One study of the top political pundits tracked all of the predictions they made about the future and determined their performance was no better than random chance. However, these people were all convinced they possessed excellent foresight. The same is true for expert stock pickers. Numerous analyses of hedge fund data reveal that you would do just as well allowing a monkey to manage your portfolio as you would hiring an MBA.

Another study of college admissions counselors investigated whether their predictions of students' success were any better than simply accepting the ones with the best GPAs and test scores. After spending many hours reading the student's essays, conducting interviews, combing through transcripts, and following up on letters of recommendation, the counselors were certain their estimates would be much better than simply going by the numbers. However, their predictions were actually less acurate when students' grades were assessed at the end of freshman year.

If we are pulled off the Track of Humility at the first checkpoint we will set highly unrealistic expectations for the future. Either we will expect the best or fear the worst. We expect to be able to drive to work in 20 minutes and we get frustrated when the traffic doesn't cooperate. We expect to finish the report in 90 minutes and we get stressed out when it still isn't done five hours later. We expect our boss to value our contribution and award us the big promotion, then we are devastated when it goes to the new guy instead. And after another full day of unmet expectations, we expect our spouse to listen and be supportive when we get home—OK, maybe we aren't *that* naive.

In the case of Cole Rodriguez, from the introduction, he expected that he could gain quick success as a motorcycle collector because he'd been collecting cars for years. If Cole would have consulted with the right people before rushing to buy the bike, they would have pointed out his blind spot. They would have told him he was being unrealistic. However, without a panel of the right people in his corner, Cole was pulled off the Track of Humility at the first checkpoint, and it cost him a quarter of a million dollars.

The same was true for pilot Roger Peterson. He expected to be able to fly the plane that night because he'd always been able to land safely in the past. The weather that evening didn't start off too bad but was predicted to get worse, just like the math problems that started off with small numbers and quickly escalated. If the weather had been nasty earlier in the night, perhaps Roger would have said no to the assignment. But it wasn't. And he didn't stop to consult with anyone else before he decided to fly the plane. If Roger had taken a moment to slow down and talk with someone he trusted before accepting this dangerous assignment, he might have been able to keep his expectations in check and stay on the Track of Humility.

Checkpoint 2: Take Responsibility

It's hard to set realistic expectations, but it's just as tricky to take responsibility for our results when things don't work out how we'd hoped. This is the second checkpoint you'll encounter as you attempt to pursue a goal or deal with a challenge. Although we might like to think we are always rational and accurate in our attributions, we tend to distort our perceptions to protect our self-concept. We shift responsibility away from ourselves, and this pulls us off the Track of Humility.

Our self-concept is the most important schema we have. It impacts our personality, shaping how we identify ourselves and the choices we make. Our brains remember information about ourselves much better and process it more quickly than other information. For instance, when you were in grade school, do you recall a time that a bully called you stupid, or ugly, or fat? Or a time that a friend expressed gratitude to you for helping them with their homework? Or when a teacher or coach said you were really great at something (or referred to you as a worthless slacker)?

If you're like most people, at least some of these self-referential moments are vivid in your memory. However, you're probably less likely to remember what that bully wore for Halloween, what car their parents drove, or whether they ever came to school with a cast on. You might be able to remember being commended for helping a friend with homework, but can you remember what subject it was for, or what grade they received after you helped them? Getting approval from an authority figure like your coach feels amazing, but can you remember what compliments they gave to the other athletes? Chances are, your ability to recall information related to your self-concept outshines your ability to recall other memories.

This effect has been noted in a test regarding word memorization. In this study, participants were given a list of forty adjectives and a simple task. One group was asked to notice whether each word was uppercase or lowercase. Another checked to see if any of the words rhymed. A third searched for synonyms. The fourth judged whether the words were true of themselves or not. Afterwards, participants were asked to recall as many adjectives as they could. Those who had been asked to think about how the words related to themselves were able to recall more than twice as many as the next best group.

Our self-concept is incredibly salient to our brains. Because of this, we tend to skew how we internally assign responsibility for the things that happen in order to maintain a certain image of ourselves. In fact, we often go as far as distorting our perception of reality to serve ourselves. One of the most prominent examples of this is the tendency to attribute our successes to ourselves, and our failures to others.

According to studies by Snyder, Stephan, & Rosenfield, we tend to take responsibility for desired outcomes while ignoring responsibility for undesirable outcomes. We want to protect our high opinion of ourselves at all costs, so we go out of our way to attribute success to our own actions while attributing failure elsewhere. This drive to bolster our self-concept is the main force that conspires to pull us off the Track of Humility at the second checkpoint.

However, we don't all have a high opinion of ourselves to protect. For people with anxiety or depression, the opposite is often the case. These individuals tend to assume too much responsibility for failure because doing so aligns with their low self-worth. These same people will often fail to take credit for success. Getting a boost to their self-worth would be an *attack* to their self-concept, so they deflect positive appraisal.

In a study from Baumeister, Stillwell, and Wotman, the researchers analyzed participants' recounts of disputes. They asked people to describe a situation where they angered someone else, and another situation in which someone angered them. Their study highlighted a phenomenon known as the attributional bias.

When referring to themselves as perpetrators, people tended to emphasize situational factors to explain their aggressive behavior, such as not getting enough sleep the night before, or feeling overwhelmed by stress. They framed their unkind actions as isolated incidents that were understandable given the situation. They also asserted that the actions caused no lasting harm. All of these techniques are subconscious mental maneuvers designed to protect our self-image and avoid taking responsibility for acting out.

On the other hand, when participants were asked to describe a time they were the victims of an altercation, they represented the perpetrator as having significant character defects. Instead of acknowledging that the perpetrator might have been tired or stressed that day, they claimed the aggressiveness was part of the individual's personality. Therefore, it was the other person's fault that the fight started. Framing the information in this way demonstrates an interesting urge in our nature. We want to know not just why something happened, but also who is to blame. We want to shift the blame away from ourselves in order to protect our self-concept and avoid consequences. It's a defense mechanism and a mental shortcut that makes avoiding responsibility a natural habit. Finding a reasonable excuse is less harmful for our self-worth than admitting a mistake. As a result, we often veer off the Track of Humility at the second checkpoint.

Conversely, for those of us with a low self-concept we might find ourselves doing the opposite. We may adopt a victim mentality and attribute negative traits to ourselves while letting others off the hook for their mistakes. By filtering the information that comes at us and choosing what to believe and what to reject, we can maintain either an entitled mentality or a victim mindset.

Have you ever been in trouble for being late? Perhaps you slipped into the conference room after the first action item had been addressed, or showed up to your cousin's birthday party after the cake was sliced. Was your response something like "Sorry everyone, I wasn't keeping track of the time," or was it more like, "Sorry, my last work call ran late and traffic was really backed up?" We don't opt for excuses all the time, but when it's a reasonable way to get out of taking personal responsibility, we all do it occasionally.

Sometimes we'll go with an excuse that is extremely outlandish in hopes that no one will question it. I remember one of my colleagues was late to an important meeting and had no good excuse for his tardiness. So he grabbed a random lamp from someone's desk and barged in, sweating, lamp in hand. "I'm so sorry everyone," he said with desperation in his voice. He took his seat, hid the lamp under his chair, and took out his notes. No one had any idea what it was that made him late, but no one dared to ask. Saving face can turn the attributional bias into an art form.

Sadly, we see the second checkpoint appear in human history countless times. There's a "he said, she said" story for almost every conflict since the birth of writing systems. For instance, who started the First World War is still up for debate. While the shooting of Franz Ferdinand was the catalyst for war to break out, there was a lot going on in the background: the demonization of certain ethnic groups, disputes between borders, fears of land acquisitions from wealthy superpowers... Everyone wanted to blame someone else for picking up their guns and shooting.

If failing to take responsibility can wreak havoc between countries, imagine what it can do to you. Sometimes we hurt ourselves to get out of taking responsibility for negative outcomes. It's called self-handicapping and it's an act of self-sabotage. You might put a nail through your own car tire to present an excuse for being late to work, rather than admit you overslept by an hour. Commonly, people reference self-sabotaging behaviors such as staying up all night drinking before an important task, so when they underperform in the big moment, they have a way to deflect personal responsibility. It's a way to say, "I did pretty well for someone who didn't sleep last night." Referencing drinking the night before, overexerting yourself, or not getting enough sleep all are ways of dodging responsibility for poor performance. The forces at the second checkpoint are pulling us off the Track of Humility.

A study on athletes finds more instances of self-handicapping in individual sports than team sports. In team sports, athletes have a diminished sense of self-concept as success and failure are based more on group effort than individual effort. When the loss is shared, diffusion of responsibility softens the blow to our self-concept. Therefore, losing a game with a team doesn't feel as bad as losing an individual event, such as a marathon race. Team athletes tend to attribute poor performance to non self-handicapping behaviors, like a tougher opponent or not enough practice, instead of referencing drinking or poor sleep. This diffusion is good for the individuals within the boundaries of a competition, but in the day-to-day of life the second checkpoint can perpetuate unnecessary harm.

Diffusion of responsibility plays into the bystander effect. The most frequently cited real-life example of the bystander effect regards a young woman called Kitty Genovese, who was murdered in Queens, New York, in 1964, while several of her neighbors looked on. No one intervened until it was too late. Everyone assumed someone else would call the police. With a whole neighborhood watching the attack everyone had a good excuse not to jump in: "someone else will take care of it."

However, if we flip the consequence of an outcome from negative to positive, we see the human desire to take responsibility flip as well.

We are often willing to take responsibility for success that doesn't belong to us, but only when we think we can get away with it. In an experiment testing honesty, participants were asked to answer six quiz questions about music. Three were relatively easy questions for music enthusiasts. *Who is the drummer from Nirvana?* The other three were nearly impossible. *Name the town and state where Michael Jackson was born.* The quiz was held in private using a web browser that participants could use to look up the answers. They would be awarded a cash prize if they answered all six questions correctly. Afterwards, they flipped a coin. If they reported a "heads," they would win an additional prize. There was a strong correlation between those with perfect test scores and those who flipped heads. The same test was conducted in a public setting that was observed by researchers. If participants were caught cheating, they would be removed from the test. In this condition fewer people got all six questions correct. This experiment demonstrates that people are more likely to take responsibility for success they didn't earn when they think they won't get caught. In private settings, people are more likely to fall victim to the self-serving bias because they don't have anything at risk. Converging evidence shows that people tend to take credit for positive outcomes to increase their self-worth if there is evidence to back up their lie.

When Buddy Holly found himself beaten down from his crazy tour schedule, he blamed the greedy record company executives, not himself. Even though he'd sought out the tour and agreed to the schedule, he didn't think freezing to death was his fault. Instead, he blamed the circumstances on others and tried to work around them. He attributed his feelings of desperation to not sleeping enough, and used his worn out and frustrated state to self-handicap the shortsighted last-minute decision to fly during foul weather. He didn't want to take responsibility for his declining health, because then he would be admitting defeat. He was pulled off the Track of Humility at the second checkpoint, and it cost him and his two friends their lives.

If we are going to stay on the path to our goals and act with foresight, we need to be willing to take responsibility for our position regardless of what we expect the consequences to be. Coming up with excuses and transferring blame is like living in a world we wish were real, but isn't. And living in a fantasy world can have far worse consequences than the ones we currently fear owning up to. This is a hard hurdle to jump, but it's not impossible. Once again, the solution comes back to having the right people in your corner to help you see your blind spots, and I'll walk you through how to do it in Chapter 4. But first I want to introduce you to the third and final checkpoint you must clear on the way to your goals…

Checkpoint 3: Be Honest With Yourself and Others

When something doesn't go our way, we tend to dodge responsibility to protect our self-concept. On the other hand, when something good happens, we usually take credit because it boosts our ego and makes us feel we're entitled to success. However, being selective about our responsibility can create a divide within us: we only take credit for results if they make us look good. After a while, we make up so many excuses for why our behaviors don't line up with our expectations that we start to lie to ourselves. We are pulled off the Track of Humility at the second checkpoint.

We don't like feeling inadequate, but we don't like disharmony either. Conflicting concepts such as, "My way to save this company is genius," and, "Implementing my idea has only made things worse," create an uncomfortable feeling known as cognitive dissonance. To resolve this feeling, we can either adjust our behavior by saying, "I messed up and need to implement a different solution," or alter our beliefs by saing, "My idea is still genius and things will get better eventually."

Usually, we choose to believe the lie so we can maintain our sense of entitlement. This is the third checkpoint on the Track of Humility. It starts by lying to ourselves in the short term at the second checkpoint, to preserve our self-concept. But eventually we reach the third checkpoint and we start to actually believe our own lies.

According to self-awareness theory, when we focus our attention on ourselves, we tend to compare our current behavior against our internal standards. Sometimes when we make these comparisons, we realize we are not currently measuring up. Maybe we see ourselves as healthy but the bathroom scale doesn't agree. Or we might consider ourselves successful, but our bank account balance isn't cooperating. In these cases, perceiving a discrepancy between our actual and ideal selves is distressing. It reminds us that we aren't the Greek gods we like to think we are. And that hurts.

The more self-aware we are, the more inadequate these discrepancies make us feel. Just look in the mirror. No really, a study involving mirrors found that people felt significantly more distressed when exposed to self-discrepancies while gazing at their own reflections. The more self-aware we are in a given situation, the more pain we feel when we are not living up to our ideals. It's often easier to lie to ourselves than to accept the truth about our failures and shortcomings.

One way we lie to ourselves at the third checkpoint is by using distractions.

For example, Moskalenko and Heine found that people who are given false negative feedback about their performance on an intelligence test focused significantly more on playing a video in the waiting room than those who were given positive feedback. Getting a low score leads to self-discrepant feelings about one's ability to succeed. To avoid thoughts of reflection and critical evaluation, we zone out on TV and social media.

Those who feel threats to their self-concept on a regular basis tend to double down on the lies they tell themselves, rather than adjusting their self-appraisals. Munro and Stansbury made a study of attacking participants' self-concepts. Participants who wrote out self-affirming statements reacted more vehemently to criticisms of these statements than did people who wrote out statements unrelated to their beliefs. When the self-affirming statements were attacked, participants' self-concepts were threatened. Subsequently, they showed greater tendencies to seek out evidence confirming their own views or disproving alternative viewpoints. The participants with non-self-affirming statements did not fight tooth and nail to back up their statements when attacked because the attacks did not threaten their self-concept.

The psychological term for maintaining a position despite contradictory evidence is self-deception. As the name suggests, it's all about lying to yourself. We choose to leave out evidence that does not confirm our beliefs about how awesome we are. If you attribute the success of your company to your ability to continually increase sales, but your sales are actually in decline, you experience dissonance. Therefore, you have two choices: admit you have improvements to make and change your behavior, or believe that everything is going according to plan and you're still a flawless salesperson. Maybe you'll tell yourself it's just a bad quarter, things will get better. Maybe you'll decide it's the new guy's fault, he's holding you back.

The more we lie to ourselves, the more wrapped up we become in our illusions and it can even influence our memories. Researchers have documented that after participating in back-breaking bike tours cyclists had positive, nostalgic recollections of the drudgery a few months later. In the same study, vacationers returning from a holiday recalled their trip with increasingly fond memories the longer it had been since the vacation. The "Good old days" phenomenon is nothing new, and someday you'll look back on this moment with rose-tinted glasses too. We simply mis-remember the past to convince ourselves it was better, even in the face of contrary evidence. It can be self-serving to remember that you had more sex, earned more accolades, and scored higher on tests than you truly did.

Psychologists have discovered that human memory doesn't work like a movie. It doesn't record reality and play it back in exactly the same way every time. When we recall memories, we activate the parts of the brain associated with perception in addition to memory. When we relive the memory, we can alter our perception of it using the power of imagination. Then we re-encode the memory along with some new alterations, and voila, we've re-written history without even realizing it. The next time a memory is recalled, it will include a few lies that are indiscernible from the truth. And then we'll modify it a little more.

In psychological experiments, researchers have successfully inserted false events into participants' childhood memories. First the participant tells a story in as much detail as possible. Then they tell the story again and the researcher informs them whether they forgot any details or not. Unbeknownst to the participant, the researcher adds a fake detail to the story. Then the participant tells the story once more, this time incorporating the false detail into their retelling, without detecting that it's fake.

This doesn't only apply to old memories. A similar test demonstrated how these types of suggestions can magically turn yield signs into stop signs in the minds of drivers looking back on an incident. While our memories can be shaped by outside influences, our own determination to lie to ourselves can create memories that better serve us.

Various studies have documented that when the stakes are higher we become even more convinced of our false beliefs. In a study at a horse race, experimenters asked people waiting in the two-dollar-bet line to estimate how confident they were in their choices. Then they asked the same question to those leaving the counter after putting down their two bucks. Unsurprisingly, those with money on line were much more confident than they had been a few minutes earlier.

Another entertaining place to observe high-stakes self-deception is in the BigFoot hunting community. These fanatics base their lives on interacting with a mythical creature and have genuinely convinced themselves of BigFoot's existence despite a lack of evidence. If they admitted they were wrong, their identity would come crumbling down. The ego wants to protect itself, so it will ignore contrary evidence and cling to reports of BigFoot sightings, no matter how far fetched. I know a website that features organic wellness oils alongside concoctions designed to attract BigFoot. I know another where you can sign up and pay a premium to hunt with professional BigFoot trackers. The livelihood of these entrepreneurs is jeopardized the day they accept the truth that BigFoot doesn't exist.

It's easy to fall off the Track of Humility at the third checkpoint and lie to ourselves, and often we don't even realize we're doing it. Sometimes the lies are reinforced so many times, we can't remember the truth anymore. We do it because it protects us from hard feelings like dissonance, self-discrepancy, and inadequacy, but the more we lie, the more dissonant our lives become. It's a vicious cycle, and it's the final checkpoint we must overcome on our way to our goals. If you get trapped here, you'll be destined to lack foresight.

The tour managers of the Winter Dance Party were caught in checkpoint number three. They were convinced they knew what was best. If they admitted they had no idea what it was like to haul concert gear across 400 miles of ice, their identities would come crashing down. They didn't stop to consult with anyone about the tour they were scheduling. They didn't have the right people in their corner to point out their blind spots. They were wrapped up in their mental distortions, and they didn't view the plane crash as any reason to stop touring. Instead, after the crash, they offered Holly's bandmates, the Crickets, extra money to complete the tour without Holly. The Crickets completed the tour, but never saw that money.

Cole Rodriguez, on the other hand, was able to return to the Track of Humility after initially being derailed at the first checkpoint. He managed to consult with numerous John Britten experts and he realized his mistake. Instead of telling himself the experts didn't know what they were talking about, he listened to what they were telling him. Rodriguez became aware of his blind spot and learned a critical lesson. Today he's one of the world's top motorcycle collectors, and his garage of bikes is valued at over $20 million. By getting the right people in his corner, with pure motivations and proper credentials, Cole was able to get back to the Track of Humility and achieve his goal. And so can you.

The Track of Humility

When we ask who is to blame for the Day the Music Died, there is no straight answer. If the flight crew from Dwyer Flight Service hadn't acted so grandiose, the plane never would have left the ground during a blizzard. If Buddy Holly had admitted he was in over his head and taken responsibility for the horrible position he found himself in, he would have quit the tour instead of chartering the flight. If General Artists Corporation stopped lying to themselves about how awful they were at planning tours, there would have been no 400-mile days in the snow, no need to replace the tour bus four times, and no last minute flights to Moorhead, Minnesota to fill the musician's only day off.

After the plane crash, news teams rushed to report on the freak accident involving three of America's beloved celebrities. Before the authorities had a chance to notify her of his death, Buddy Holly's pregnant wife learned of his death on national TV. Her skin turned white and she couldn't breathe. The revelation was so unreal, so mortifying, that she never truly recovered. Shortly afterward, María Elena Holly suffered a miscarriage.

The Victim's Rights policy was subsequently adopted and it now states that victims' names cannot be disclosed in the media until after their families had been informed of the incident. This practice is still in effect today.

Getting trapped at these three checkpoints on the path to your goals won't necessarily lead to the loss of life or the passing of new legislation, but it can ruin your self-image and destroy your personal relationships. You can still achieve some success without getting past the checkpoints, but your life will likely feel unfulfilled. It's easy to get trapped at the checkpoints, but it won't take you where you truly want to be.

The checkpoints are challenging, but they are not impossible to overcome.

While we are susceptible to falling into these traps, we don't need to be vulnerable to our own destruction. We don't have to let the wiring of our lazy, self-preserving, and egotistical brains dictate all of our thoughts and actions. We can resist the traps by getting the right people in our corner. What we need is to find a panel of personal advisors with the right motivations and credentials to point out our blind spots and keep us on the path to our goals.

There are a few simple techniques you can use to find the right people to advise you and keep yourself on the Track of Humility, and we'll get into those in Chapter 4. But first, we need to talk about why it's so easy to fall into these three traps. The big problem is overinvestment. We move into things too quickly and we get too wrapped up in them. The solution is to follow the 20% Rule, which we will tackle in the next chapter.

Chapter 2
The Danger of Success

When the forces at any of the three checkpoints pull us off the Track of Humility, we're at risk of falling down the treacherous spiral of disillusionment. The farther off the Track of Humility we fall, the more our perception of reality begins to deviate from the truth. When this disillusionment becomes unavoidable, our downward spiral hits rock bottom. We find ourselves in a pit of despair, chock-full of excuses, and we become discredible.

As we strive to achieve our goals, we must pass safely through the three checkpoints. This will help us develop the imagination, values, and efficiency required to have 20/20 foresight. If we don't have the right people in our corner to keep us on the Track of Humility then we are doomed to slip up, and the downward spiral of disillusionment can be a challenging trend to reverse. It's a trend psychologists have been puzzled by long before disillusionment caused the catastrophe on The Day the Music Died.

One of the most notable studies on disillusionment happened in the winter of 1955 when Leon Festinger and some fellow observers infiltrated a doomsday cult called The Seekers. These members believed that their leader had been receiving messages from aliens. The friendly extraterrestrials explained that the world was going to be obliterated in a flood, and that The Seekers could be saved on the morning of the predicted disaster, December 21, 1955.

To Festinger's amazement, after the day of the apocalypse came and went, the cult members didn't abandon their beliefs. In fact, some of them doubled down. Members who had given up their belongings and friendships to prepare for the alien arrival sought media attention after the failed prophecy to justify their beliefs and convince others to join The Seekers. This baffled Festinger. What could cause people to persist in a disillusioned view of reality in the face of overwhelming contradictory evidence?

His research revealed that the answer has to do with an individual's level of investment.

The Twenty Percent Rule

Some illusions can cause us to embark on a self-destructive music tour. Others can take hold of us and compel us to stand around a prophet's living room waiting for an astronaut to shuttle us to a flying saucer. The more invested we become in these beliefs the harder it is to let them go, even in the face of contrary evidence.

For example, think of the last time an advertisement got the best of you. Maybe it was a travel ad, or a commercial for a new phone plan, or perhaps it was a fast food campaign. We've all seen those slow-motion close-ups of the juiciest, most delicious hamburger ever created. It's hard not to drool at the scared ground beef, fluffy golden buns, toppings stacked high, and sauce dripping from the edges of the sandwich. Steam comes off the hot patty pressed up against the veggies that are somehow still cool enough to attract condensation. Then we order the damn thing and it's nothing like we thought. It's flat, soggy, and lacking luster. It's messy, and not in a good way. It might taste okay, but it's nothing like the burger in the ads. The million-dollar advertisement made by professional filmmakers is nothing close to the three-dollar item from the value menu.

In the case of the fake burger commercial it's easy for us to adjust our beliefs when we are faced with reality. The main reason is because we aren't overinvested in the food being good. We aren't a spokesperson for fast food. We haven't gone around telling all of our friends, "Hey this is the best burger in town!" We have nothing at stake. When there's nothing riding on maintaining the illusion, we can yield to new evidence that counters it.

However, when we are more heavily invested in a way of thinking or behaving it can be much more difficult to weed out our inaccuracies. Without proper foresight and people in our corner to help us identify blindspots, we can build our entire lives upon illusions. When we do, even evidence that we are wrong isn't enough to change our beliefs. In fact, when an illusion is deep enough contradictory evidence can actually strengthen it further.

The difference between an impenetrable illusion and a paper thin one is our level of investment. When we reach the point of being overly invested in something, changing our mind becomes twice as hard as sticking the course, even when we know we're clearly wrong. For this reason, there's a tipping point, and if we move past this point we will be especially likely to fall off the Track of Humility into one of the three pitfalls. This tipping point is 20% emotional investment. Here's why...

A Bird in the Hand

They say a bird in the hand is worth two in the bush, and they're right (whoever 'they' are). It's possible this saying originally came from John Ray, who used the phrase in his 1670 compilation of proverbs. Or it might have come from the Bible, specifically Ecclesiastes 9:4, which states that "A living dog is better than a dead lion." Regardless, it's a saying that's stuck around— and for a good reason. It's psychologically accurate. Modern scientific research has tested this ancient idiom and confirmed that gaining one bird is equivalent to losing two.

Hundreds of studies in fields ranging from behavioral economics, to game theory, to social psychology have reached universal agreement on this magical ratio. The human brain really does treat losses as twice as impactful as gains. If you purchased a coffee for one dollar, and were about to raise it to your lips when someone offered to buy it from you for a dollar, would you sell it? Most people would sell it for two dollars, but not one. Some studies have found this effect trickling all the way down to a single nickel. In experimental settings, people are twice as torn up about a five cent surcharge as they are about gaining five cents as a bonus.

In a study from 1991, participants were given a mug and then offered the chance to sell it or trade it for some equally valued pens. The researchers found the amount of pens participants required as compensation for a mug was about twice as high as the amount they were willing to pay to acquire the mug. However, this effect was only present *after* participants had claimed ownership of the mug.

In 1984, Knetsch and Sinden demonstrated this effect with unmistakable accuracy. In their study, participants were awarded either a lottery ticket or two dollars. Later, each subject was offered an opportunity to trade the lottery ticket for the money, or vice versa. Very few subjects chose to switch. In this case, both prizes increased in value for no other reason than that they were in the hand instead of in the bush. Hanging on to the prizes caused them to double in perceived value, regardless of what they were.

Further research has demonstrated that we will accept larger risks to avoid losses than to achieve gains—even when both have equivalent value. We will work twice as hard to avoid losing $500 than we will to gain $500. This is because, psychologically, the loss feels twice as painful to us as the gain feels good. Even though the actual value of the loss and gain are exactly the same ($500), the subjective value, or the way they feel, is different.

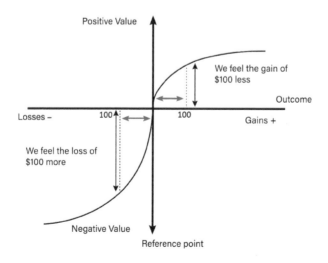

Losses affect us twice as much as gains.

In one study, people were tasked with completing anagrams and they were rewarded in two different ways. One group was given $4 and told they could earn an extra dollar if they solved the final puzzle. The other group was given $5 and told they would lose $1 if they failed to solve the final puzzle. Of course, these scenarios are the same, just phrased in different ways. But the results were striking.

Participants worked much harder to avoid losing a dollar than they did to earn a dollar. The final puzzle, it turns out, was impossible. The researchers simply wanted to see how long people would persist at it before giving up. And the ones who were told they would lose a dollar for failing to complete the puzzle worked much longer than the ones who were told they would gain a dollar. They cared twice as much about the loss of a dollar than they did about the gain.

Loss aversion has its benefits. In another study, researchers hypothesized that people with higher stakes might be more likely to quit an unhealthy habit. The results were astounding. Over a six month period of time, three groups of smokers were challenged to stop smoking. The first group, a control group, was given six months' worth of free nicotine patches to encourage the cessation of their habit. Only 6% succeeded. The second group, the "Reward Group," was told that if they could stop smoking for six months then they would be given an $800 reward. In this group 17% of participants were successful. Then there was the third group, the "Deposit Group."

Participants in the "Deposit Group" paid $150 at the start of the trial and were told that if they completed six months without smoking they would receive their $150 back as well as an additional $650 reward. Even though the total possible reward for their time was $150 less than that of the reward group, participants worked much harder to break their habit. The success rate in this group was 52%! This is the power of loss aversion. And it doesn't just apply to money, it happens with emotions too.

In 1995, the American Psychological Association was fascinated by the 1992 Summer Olympics held in Barcelona, Spain. They weren't drawn in by the gorgeous scenery and fierce competition as much as they were by the awards ceremonies. A team of researchers was looking to gauge the impressions of the bronze medalists compared to the silver medalists.

The APA found that bronze medalists were significantly happier to get on the pedestal than silver medalists, even though they had lower scores in their events. Interviews confirmed this discrepancy. Many bronze medalists framed third place as gaining an award rather than losing out entirely. Even third place beats fourth place by a longshot. On the other hand, silver medalists framed second place as losing out on the gold. They didn't experience a win, they experienced a loss. Despite beating the bronze medalists, they were disappointed. In this case, we can see that loss aversion applies with emotional investments just as it does with financial investments. Losing feels twice as bad as winning feels good.

These experiments demonstrate that we place much more value on avoiding a loss than we do on achieving a gain. Truly, a bird in the hand is worth two in the bush. Less is more when there's a loss at stake. This phenomenon explains why it's so hard to stay on the Track of Humility and pass through the checkpoints. Once we become invested in a certain outcome we'll readily deceive ourselves to avoid the emotional pain of failure.

Negativity Bias

Losses don't have to come in the form of cash or Olympic medals to be impactful. Sometimes, losses aren't tangible at all. When we make emotional investments in beliefs and ideas, we are risking our self-image. Therefore, we value our beliefs more highly when our self-image is at stake. We are averse to losing credibility, esteem, or status. Even when we are proven wrong on a bad investment, many of us will still hang on to our plummeting stock, clinging to a false belief. Sometimes we'll even invest more. It's easier to believe there is still hope than it is to accept the reality of a loss. This is what happened with the doomsday cult that Festinger observed.

Humans attach more meaning to bad experiences than to good ones. This is because negativity bias gives us an evolutionary edge. The idea of climbing a mountain might sound nice, but the thought of falling or being bitten by a snake is more than enough to dissuade most potential hikers from risking their lives. Positive experiences are nice, but negative experiences can be life ending!

Studies have suggested that negativity bias shows up in babies around seven months of age. This means it's likely that our tendency towards negativity bias is inborn. Bad is stronger than good. Kids aren't better behaved in December because they are excited by the reward of gifts, but because they fear a misstep might relegate them to Santa's naughty list and prevent them from getting gifts. And while belief in Santa Claus might disappear with age, the tendency to assign greater importance to negative experiences than positive ones does not.

Without the right people in our corner to keep us on the Track of Humility, we are at a disadvantage to combat negativity bias. We will bend and break our perception of reality to avoid having to face the hard truth. We give the fear of pain more credit than it deserves, and this hinders us from exercising foresight. This is why we need a boundary to proactively protect ourselves from overinvesting emotionally in anything and being pulled off the Track of Humility.

The Perfect Investment

When you combine loss aversion theory with the negativity bias, you can see that the more of ourselves we invest into anything the harder it becomes to walk away. Even when evidence tells us our investment is not good.

That's why I live by the 20% emotional reserve rule.

If losses are twice as impactful as gains, then investing 20% of your emotional energy into anything means a loss could wipe out 40% of your emotional reserves. That doesn't feel good, but at least it leaves more than half of our emotional state intact. The loss will hurt, but we will still have 60% of our emotional fortitude left to help us recover. However, investing 25% of our energy or more means we risk losing at least 50% of our self-worth. In this case, the majority of your emotional stamina could be drained by a single loss. This leaves you fragile and susceptible to burnout.

My friend John Bowers once told me, "when you deceive, what a tangled web you weave." It's true that our subconscious mind can weave a web of deception, which makes it very difficult to see an accurate reflection in the mirror. But if you invest no more than 20% of your emotions in everything you do, you will not feel compelled to weave a web of lies to protect yourself. This helps you stay on the Track of Humility, even in the face of failure. When you get overinvested, on the other hand, a single setback can completely derail you.

The Path of Failure

Every illusion starts at the first checkpoint, with a misalignment between expectations and reality. Typically, we buy into an illusion when we are over-confident about the future and lack foresight. We think we've got something figured out, but we don't. This is how we are pulled into the **Grandiose Mindset**.

We fall into grandiosity on a regular basis because sometimes it's natural to be optimistic. When we plan a trip to the coast, we hope the good weather will hold up. When we enter a contest, we pray we'll come out on top. When we experience a great date with a new romantic partner, we're optimistic the good times will keep rolling. If we successfully refrain from investing over 20% of our emotional reserve into these expectations, we will be able to go back to the drawing board without deluding ourselves. If clouds start to form, we'll call off the coastline trip or pack an umbrella. But if we're overly invested we might refuse to believe that rain is coming. When we confront reality, we can observe the truth and respond to it. But when we're more than 20% tied up in something we won't be able to see reality. The key is not allowing ourselves to become emotionally overinvested in the first place. That's how we stay on the **Track of Humility**.

However, if we do invest over 20% of our emotional reserves, we fall victim to inflated expectations and slide into the Grandiose Mindset. In fact, it's more likely that we will make the error of running head first into a test when we feel overconfident. This is due to a variety of psychological factors.

Going Head First

What gives us the confidence to run head first into a challenge when the reality is that we are underprepared and uninformed? One factor is the surprisingly positive effect confidence has on improving performance under pressure. When our confidence is backed up by actual skills it's a good thing. But when we are unrealistically confident it's a form of inflated expectations and a symptom of the Grandiose Mindset.

One study asked participants to shoot fifteen basketballs from the free throw line in two rounds. There was nothing special about the first round, simply take a shot and see if it goes in the basket. For the second round, the basketball players were being videotaped to add an element of pressure. When the pressure was on, the participants who believed in themselves worked harder and performed better.

Performing a difficult task under pressure makes overconfident players shine and unconfident players crack. This fascinating trend is partially why we dive head first into challenges in which we think we will exceed, even if we lack the proper skills. This can cause problems.

If you were under the illusion that you were an amazing singer you might audition for a talent show such as *America's Got Talent* for a shot at the big time. Yet, your expectations are unrealistic and so you'll be rejected. If you invested less than 20% of your emotional reserves in being a singer, you might take the rejection in stride. If you invested more than 20% of your emotional reserves in being a singer by posting about it on social media, shelling out money for a plane ticket to the audition, and dropping out of school to pursue your talent, the rejection could wipe you out. When the judges boo you offstage your world could come crashing down.

When you are emotionally overinvested in something and fail, you fall into the **Despair Mindset**. You did not live up to your expectations. You begin to feel nothing will ever work out for you. Your life is over and it seems there's no going back. However, there is a way back.

Start by dusting yourself off with the help of your advisors (who you carefully selected). Take responsibility for your choices that brought you this failure, and admit that you were trapped in a grandiose fantasy. Assess the mistake, the people that were involved, the approach, and every other conceivable factor for why the mission failed. This is an opportunity to prepare yourself to try again.

Remember, getting back on the Track of Humility is crucial. It is very important for you to put aside your emotional state and revisit why you failed in a humble state of mind, because that way you can reattach yourself to what you're trying to do. From a place of humility you can methodically make choices that will allow you to cross that finish line. It is the energy between grandiosity and despair that will keep you balanced, on target, and on the **Track of Humility**.

Bouncing back from failure is not easy. If you were overinvested emotionally in being a singer then accepting the judges' criticism could destroy your self-worth. To avoid this loss, you might instead decide to reject their feedback and fall into a second trap, the **Excuses** trap. At this stage, you don't want to admit a loss so you invent an explanation for your failure and shift the blame away from yourself. We all know what these excuses sound like:

I'm an amazing singer, they don't know what they're talking about. Who elected those judges in the first place? I'd like to see them try to do what I can do. They wouldn't know talent if it bit them in the butt!

Or,

My vocal chords were too tight because my singing instructor pushed me too hard this week. If my neighbors weren't up late making noise I would have gotten better sleep and I would have performed better. Venus was in retrograde and that's really bad luck for my astrological sign. It wasn't my fault.

As long as we continue to keep a high personal investment in singing, we will continue to blame everyone around us in a desperate attempt to protect our self-worth. Failing at something when we're overinvested causes us to slide from the Grandiose Mindset to the Despair Mindset if we accept the failure and to the Excuses Mindset if we reject the failure.

Thankfully all is not yet lost. We can backtrack all the way to the Track of Humility. But it will take a lot out of us to make this journey. Admitting our expectations were unrealistic isn't fun when we're heavily invested. The better way to avoid the Excuses Mindset is to keep our emotional investment under 20% from the beginning and stay on the Track of Humility. This way we can create realistic expectations based upon sound research and advice.

But what if you did somehow manage to impress the *America's Got Talent* judges? What if you moved onto the next round despite having unrealistic expectations about your singing abilities? What if you experienced a success instead of a failure when you put your Grandiose Mindset to the test? We tend to think it's better to succeed than to fail, but early success can actually be more dangerous because Beginner's Luck can give us a false sense of expertise. Early success is dangerous when we're operating in an illusion...

The Path of Early Success

When you approach something with a Grandiose Mindset and you actually end up succeeding you'll find yourself pulled into the **Entitlement Mindset**. This makes you think you were prepared all along and your success is clear evidence of your superior ability. The problem here is that you're inappropriately assigning a successful process to a successful outcome. You can get out of the Entitlement Mindset and return to the Track of Humility if you realize that you should never stop working to refine your process. This is easier to do if you avoid investing more than 20% of your emotional reserve in anything. If you're highly invested and experience a string of successes, you may use those to validate your illusion of grandiosity, putting you into the Entitlement Mindset.

One way to demonstrate the confusion between a successful outcome and a successful process is through the clustering illusion. Take a look at the following data of boys and girls who are in line for the register as I write this chapter from a busy public cafe.

Dataset 1:
Boy, Girl, Boy, Boy, Girl, Boy, Girl, Girl, Girl, Boy, Boy, Girl

Dataset 2:
Boy, Boy, Boy, Boy, Boy, Boy, Girl, Girl, Girl, Girl, Girl, Girl

One of these datasets is completely made up. Can you tell which one?

Most people are inclined to say that dataset 2 is fabricated because it's highly unlikely that six boys would cluster together followed by six girls. This is

entirely untrue. Any statistician would know that true randomness in a fifty-fif-
ty split can result in either dataset 1 or 2 with the same probability. Yet, since
we are biased to believe that one cluster of data can be more significant, is this
case signaling that dataset two is made up?

What if we were to rewrite the dataset like this:

Dataset 1:
Fail, Success, Fail, Fail, Success, Fail, Success, Success, Success, Fail, Fail

Dataset 2:
Fail, Fail, Fail, Fail, Fail, Fail, Success, Success, Success, Success, Success

Both datasets have a 50% success rate, yet when we experience a cluster
of successes, it makes us think that we're doing better than we were before. We
overestimate our abilities and think there must have been some change that
is making us successful. However, this is confusing a successful process with a
successful outcome.

The 50% success rate in dataset 2 appears to demonstrate that a change
occurred between the string of failures and the string of successes, therefore
if we keep doing what we're doing, we will experience more success in the
future. However, these outcomes are not indicative of a successful process. A
successful process would yield a higher success rate than 50%.

Experiencing success reinforces the illusion that we're talented, so we ar-
en't prompted to make adjustments to improve our process. Instead, we tend
to rest on our laurels, confident our overestimation is a realistic expectation.

A look at stock portfolios finds that traders who experienced the greatest
losses were the ones who experienced early successes. They got in at the right
time, saw rapid growth of their investments, and believed they had the market
all figured out. These successes pushed them from the Grandiose Mindset
into the Entitlement Mindset. They confused their successful outcome with a
successful process and bet more money on their false beliefs, leading to bigger
losses in the long run.

These examples of the clustering illusion feed into a greater bias known as confirmation bias. Confirmation bias is when you overplay evidence that confirms your preexisting beliefs and underplay evidence that contradicts your preexisting beliefs. This is basically the "See, I told you so!" effect and further inhibits our ability to make healthy evaluations. The stock traders who lost out in the long run might not have seen an issue in their process because they were anchored on the early successes and overlooked their deeper issues. They viewed a string of successes as proof of their superiority and they got cocky as a result.

You begin to see the world the way you expect it to look instead of how it actually looks. We can see the power expectations have on perception if we look at the McGurk effect. Or rather, if we *hear* the McGurk effect. If you were to look up this effect on the Internet right now you would see a strange video of a man staring at the camera saying "Bah, Bah, Bah, Bah." then switching to "Fah, Fah, Fah, Fah."

Except he didn't switch syllables at all. The audio from the Bah segment is identical to the audio from the Fah segment. What changed was the video feed. It went from a clip of a man saying Bah to a clip of a man saying Fah. We can see how his lips make a completely different movement. The unmistakable lower lip movement of an "Eff" sound signals our brain to perceive Fah when the audio is really saying Bah the whole time. We expect a different mouth movement will create a different sound. So we actually *hear* something that's not even there!

The most curious thing about the McGurk effect is that being aware of it does not save you from it. Even the experimenters who study the effect report they cannot hear a "Bah" sound during the Fah segment unless they close their eyes. Expectations are so influential on how we perceive reality that knowing how an illusion works does not always prevent us from perceiving it.

If you've spent much time in the Entitlement Mindset, you're likely perceiving your illusion as reality. You're probably resisting constructive criticism. You might start building your life around your success, putting more eggs in the illusion basket. To avoid fear of looking phony or foolish, you might double down and reject attacks to your illusion or recruit others to buy into the illusion too, like the doomsday cult members did after the failed prophecy. The more you deflect, the more you convince yourself of the lies and ignore underlying inadequacies.

If you invest too heavily in your illusion, your well being and identity depend on maintaining it. Even if you experience a cluster of successes that reinforce your illusion, you're bound to run into contrary evidence sooner or later.

There's a story behind the Chinese idiom "lan yu chong shu" that speaks to the effects of an ongoing illusion. Lan yu chong shu roughly translates to "a bad yu to add up the numbers" and refers to a yu player named Nan Guo who faked his way into the royal court of the Qi King. A yu is a sort of flute that Nan Guo couldn't play very well, but learned how to mimic with great mastery. In a group of other yu players, he seemed to play flawlessly. So flawlessly, that he became a yu player for the king. This plays into a cognitive bias called honor by association. When we perceive a group as generally good, we attribute that goodness to its members, even when we shouldn't. It's the opposite of a better known effect called guilty by association, in which we attribute guilt to someone associated with a certain group, even if that individual had nothing to do with the offense.

Nan Guo invested his whole life in the illusion that he was a masterful yu player and lived a lavish life as a result. He was in so deep, he would maintain the illusion at all costs. When the Qi King died and his son took the throne, Nan Guo was in trouble. The new king preferred solo performances.

Nan Guo was way over the 20% rule and had fallen into the Entitlement Mindset, believing he had it all figured out. But there was no way he could deal with the contrary evidence of failing to play the yu in a solo setting before the king. To protect his ego, he rejected the possibility of failure by fleeing the kingdom, never to be seen or heard from again. Lan yu chong shu, he's a bad yu player when you add up the evidence.

When your luck runs out and you face contrary evidence, you have two choices: Accept the evidence or reject it.

If you can get past the Entitlement Mindset without investing too much, you might be able to accept contrary evidence. However this is often not the case. Early success encourages future investments of over 20% because running in head first worked in the past. It takes a lot of emotional fortitude to admit you were wrong after a series of successes when new evidence comes to light.

Nonetheless, if you can stay under 20% emotionally invested and accept contrary evidence, you're back on the **Track of Humility**.

When your emotional investment is over 20% and you actively use your ego as a protective mechanism to reject contrary evidence to guard your self-worth, you're propelled into the **Charlatan Mindset**. A charlatan is someone who is convinced they are more proficient in a specific subject than they actually are.

There is also a third interaction that can occur when faced with contrary evidence. What if you're under 20% emotionally invested and still reject the evidence? At this point you've become **Discreditable**. You've neither convinced yourself nor others that the contrary evidence is false. You feel it's more convenient to move forward on a false-positive (a lie) than to take a step back and forge through that checkpoint. It's easier to be right than to do the right thing.

There are very famous liars known for rejecting evidence just for the sake of it. Fake news promoters. Tabloid writers. Internet trolls. They are all discreditable. Their lies merely exist to add false information that stirs the pot and gets attention. Their audience can never tell if they're being truthful or not, yet these liars never invest heavily in their positions. They'll switch sides on an issue when it's beneficial to do so. They'll find some reason to value lies over truth until they've lost all trust and respect. They've become comfortable with cognitive dissonance of being serial liars.

It's challenging to get back to the **Track of Humility** from the Discreditable Mindset or the Charlatan Mindset. The only way to do so is to backtrack to the contrary evidence, accept it, and avoid falling into the Grandiose Mindset by respecting the 20% barrier. Escaping from the Charlatan Mindset could challenge personal relationships, our ego, emotional wellbeing, our trust, and respect of self and others. Most people are averse to a loss of that magnitude. We've made a decision prematurely and don't want to admit we were wrong to begin with.

Getting Under 20%

The best way to stay out of the Grandiose Mindset is to avoid investing more than 20% of our emotional reserve in anything. Protecting this 20% rule is extremely valuable to our relationships with ourselves, family members, friends, and coworkers. This 20% rule is not to be taken lightly. Many people are willing to give up a piece of who they are for another person. That's self-sabotage. Don't give more than 20% to anything.

The 20% rule is a boundary that gives us a margin of safety when emotionally engaging in anything. This guarded 20% becomes a part of our identity and our emotional and psychological welfare. And most importantly, keeping it secure helps us stay out of the Grandiose Mindset.

Other people's behavior will demonstrate what they're really telling you more than their words. When you see what they are doing, believe that, not their words. And when they say one thing and do another, focus more on the behavior than what they say, because those are the red flags that should caution you from emotionally engaging with and investing in this type of person. This is a vampire that will suck your energy and spirit alive. Staying under 20% emotionally prevents us from making any single person the center of our entire world.

The movie *The Room* is wildly famous because Tommy Wiseau overvalued his own story, acting, and directing skills. He thought it would be a smash hit, so he spent his whole life savings, his sanity, and his identity to produce the film. He didn't trust anyone else to pull off his creative visions successfully, so he controlled every aspect of production. He deflected constructive criticism and contrary evidence. He built everything on this illusion and convinced himself that it was the greatest piece of cinema ever created. In reality, he made one of the worst films of all time.

Upon viewing *The Room* Tommy Wiseaus' charlatanism is palpable and laughable. So much so, it's a cult classic film known around the world. It made Tommy Wiseau's entire career even though he's a laughing stock. In 2017, Seth Rogan and James Franco released *The Disaster Artist*, an adaptation of the making of *The Room*, which further ridicules, yet popularizes Wiseau. *The*

Disaster Artist made 1.2 million dollars on opening day. *The Room* made $1,900 in its first two weeks. Living in an illusion can pay off, but no one will take you seriously.

You'll know you're a charlatan if your relationships start failing, you lose the trust and respect of others, and you can't feel happy with yourself. The best way to avoid these pitfalls is to resist investing more than 20% of your emotional reserve in anything in the first place. If you can dodge the Grandiose Mindset at the first Checkpoint, you'll stay on the Track of Humility where you can easily pass through the next two checkpoints.

If you're in too deep with your investment and find yourself caught in one of the pitfalls, you're not doomed. There's always a path back to the Track of Humility. There's a way to get your ego in check and become okay with loss instead of averse to it. Instead of burying your inadequacies with illusions, you must understand them...

Chapter 3
Filling The Void

Pursuing a difficult goal is a bit like walking through a minefield. Staying on the ideal path means using foresight to dodge the pitfalls. We risk falling off the Track of Humility when we fail to pass through any of the three checkpoints.

The first checkpoint appears when we set our expectations. Realistic expectations will keep us on the Track of Humility. When we overestimate our abilities, we can fall into the Grandiose Mindset and overinvest emotionally. This is a risky situation. Imagine being an understudy for the role in a Broadway musical, but not practicing your lines because you thought you knew them like the back of your hand. Suddenly, the lead actor falls ill and you have to fill in. You find yourself under the spotlight without knowing what to say. If you crash and burn, you might think you'll never work in show business again. If you manage to pull off the performance with seamless improvisation, you might think you're the best actor on the block.

Both outcomes are pitfalls that lead you further from the Track of Humility and into illusion. To get past the first checkpoint without falling into a trap, you must set realistic expectations. However, this is easier said than done and, as we will explore in Chapter 4, it often requires the assistance of some trusted people in your corner.

The second checkpoint arises out of the blame game. This is induced by the trap of Entitlement. Who's fault is it that the understudy didn't rehearse their lines? To stay on the Track of Humility if you were the understudy, you would have to take responsibility for your actions and say, "Yeah, I really messed up there. I should take my job more seriously. Even though I got away with it, this is no way to treat the role of understudy." However, it's easy to come up with excuses to protect your self-concept.

Instead of owning up to your mistake, you might say, "Well, it's the actor's fault for getting sick. I didn't know I was going to have to go on stage tonight. Otherwise I would have brushed up on my lines." That's when you fall off the straight and narrow into a pitfall. It might propel you from Grandiose to Entitlement, or from Despair to Excuses. If you don't own up to your actions you won't compel yourself to recognize the inadequacy and memorize your lines. Instead, you'll stay in the illusion.

Checkpoint three shows up when you start to convince yourself of your own lies. In the face of contrary evidence you will be so resolute in your pre-existing opinion that you double down on it. When you make enough Excuses and say "it's not fair" enough times, you begin to believe deep down that you are a victim. You'll hold this as true even when the director of the play points out that you left your copy of the script in the dressing room all week... And you haven't been *in* the dressing room since last month. Why would you? It's not like you needed stage makeup as an understudy. Continuing to believe that you're not at fault when the evidence suggests otherwise makes you a Charlatan. Soon or later you will lose the respect of others, which earns you the reputation of being discreditable.

We fall into these traps for a variety of reasons, but we perpetuate the illusion when we are over-invested. The Twenty Percent Rule states that giving more than 20% of yourself emotionally to one thing or another is an over-investment because it prevents you from admitting your faults. Loss aversion theory finds that losses are about twice as impactful as gains are exciting. Therefore, an investment of over 20% risks greater than a 40% loss of who you are. Should you find yourself overinvested and off the Track of Humility, taking responsibility and admitting your shortcomings will feel like too great a toll. That's one of the reasons why we maintain illusions. But it's not the only reason.

Overinvesting and falling into traps has another governing force called the Dark, Negative Attitude. This emerges from our reactions to misalignments in our lives. When we notice a misalignment between how things are and how we want them to be, it creates a void. Understanding why there is a misalignment can help us stay on the right track and avoid stepping on any landmines. However, trying to fill the void without understanding where the misalignment came from reinforces illusions and distortions. In this chapter I'll explain how it all works, and why we need people in our corner to help us stay aware of our blindspots and avoid pitfalls. But first, we have to define the void.

Defining the Void

The void is a misalignment in your life. It's like looking at your reflection in a shattered mirror. One shard of glass reflects your eyes and forehead while another reflects your nose and lips. The two images don't quite line up. Your ear is where your cheek should be and your nose isn't between your eyes. Your reflection resembles a Picasso or a Mondrian instead of the Mona Lisa it should be. If you close one eye, squint, and tilt your head to the side you can somewhat line up the edges of your portrait until it appears to be an accurate representation, but you're only fooling yourself.

The void is like this shattered mirror. To understand the void we have to acknowledge that it's broken and replace it. Unfortunately our first instinct is to try to fill the void, which is impossible.

The void is a fundamental disconnect between two related parts. Like tilted shards of a mirror, or a boxcar with incompatible couplings that won't link to the rest of the train.

There are four types of misalignments we can experience:

1. The misalignment of our <u>expectations</u> and our <u>realities</u>
2. The misalignment of our <u>values</u> and our <u>behaviors</u>
3. The misalignment of our <u>wants</u> and our <u>goals</u>
4. The misalignment of what we perceive as a <u>need</u> versus a <u>want</u>

To understand the void created by these misalignments, we often need the additional perspectives of carefully selected people in our corner. As a team we can figure out why the mirror is broken and what we can do to fix it. We see the misalignment for what it is and stay on the Track of Humility. We'll dive deep into this in Part 2. Right now, let's work to understand the void and the Dark, Negative Attitude.

When we aim to fill the void, we operate with the Dark, Negative Attitude. When the Dark, Negative Attitude dominates our outlook, we view ourselves and others in a distorted way. What we see in the mirror is not necessarily realistic. We manipulate the distortion to force alignment out of misalignment. This takes us off the Track of Humility and into illusions and pitfalls. I'll explain the relationship between filling the void and falling into traps after I define the Dark, Negative Attitude.

Defining the Dark, Negative Attitude

Each of us has a mixture of two different attitudes inside: light and dark. Imagine the yin-yang symbol, presenting two opposing energies in harmony. Except our light and dark attitudes are never perfectly balanced like that.

The popular *Star Wars* saga describes the Force as having a light side and a dark side. As kids grow up there is a time when one side dominates the other. At this point the kid becomes either a Jedi or a Sith. Likewise, within each of us one Attitude will overpower the other and become the default Attitude.

If we let the Dark, Negative Attitude dominate, we will view ourselves in a distorted way. We will have a corrupted imagination, inadequate values, and inefficient actions that perpetuate our downward spiral of disillusionment. We will do the wrong things for the wrong reasons in the wrong ways. We will have an unhealthy self-image and react to misalignments in an unhealthy manner. To compensate for this, we'll let ourselves fall into traps.

Imagine your neighbor drives home in a luxurious red Mercedes to celebrate his quite large signing bonus at the new law firm in town. You applied for the same position without knowing you were competing against the Joneses. You feel you're just as qualified as Mr. Jones, but you're not the one with the shiny new car. There's no mistaking it. You weren't selected and he was. There are a few ways you might react.

Admiration: *I want to be like my neighbor because he's doing well. He probably has more experience than I do, so he earned the position fair and square. I know I'm a decent lawyer and if I work harder at it, I might have what he has someday. Good for him.*

Responding with admiration is a hallmark of the Track of Humility. You're happy to see others succeed and it doesn't make you feel left out. Your values help you retain a strong sense of self-respect. You're inspired to be proactive and do good work so you can be in a similar position yourself. Above all, you stay on the Track of Humility.

Jealousy: *I'll never amount to my neighbor because he's better than me. He probably got the job because he's better looking and funnier. I'm not as charming in interviews. And my resume doesn't hold a candle to his. I should stop applying to other firms. Maybe I'm not cut out to be a top-notch lawyer.*

The Dark, Negative Attitude might influence you to experience jealousy when Mr. Jones does well. This will take the wind out of your sails and leave you feeling self-doubt, insecurity, and despair. Instead of focusing on what you can do to earn a car like that, with this response you're being reactive. You lack carefully selected values and supporters to anchor you to the Track of Humility. Your mood is dependent on what Mr. Jones does, not what you do (or don't do). This leads you into the Despair Mindset and reinforces the Dark, Negative Attitude.

Envy: *I hate my neighbor because he's successful and I'm not. I deserved the position because I'm better than him. I bet he had some inside information or something. That's the only reason he could've beaten me. I can't relate to his success, so I want him to fail.*

Envy is another emotion that comes with the Dark, Negative Attitude. Like jealousy, envy is experienced when you lack a support network rooting you to the Track of Humility. It's an example of reactivity instead of proactivity. Envy is also a sign of a corrupted imagination. Rather than consider how to achieve what Joneses achieved, an envious person would focus on the present fact that they are not successful already. They would use that negative emotion as fuel for disillusionment instead of a warning sign they are sliding off the Track of Humility. This permits the envious person to maintain an illusion of grandeur without developing the skills necessary for a desired outcome. Thus, they will be pulled into the Grandiose Mindset.

Jealousy and envy aren't the only emotions associated with the Dark, Negative Attitude. There are dozens of temperaments that promote unhealthy reactions such as inadequacy, fear, dissatisfaction, hatred, loathing, pity, and despair.

The more you react to circumstances with unhealthy emotions, the more dominant the Dark, Negative Attitude becomes. Why do we get wrapped up in this attitude so easily? Doesn't everyone know beating yourself up doesn't accomplish anything?

We operate with the Dark, Negative Attitude to distort our misalignments and fill the void. The Dark, Negative Attitude is enticing when we're insecure and refuse to take responsibility for our inadequacies. It's easier to deflect and avoid our own shortcomings than to do the hard work of changing for the better. It feels better to righteously judge others than it does to work on self-improvement.

Operating with the Dark, Negative Attitude can have its upsides. For some, living this way works out fine. However, even if things appear to be going well the Dark, Negative Attitude causes people's lives to grow more misaligned and the void grows larger as their self-image declines. To compensate, such people heavily distort their lives and fall into more pitfalls. Attempting to fill the void instead of understanding it leads them off the Track of Humility and into lives of illusion.

How can we better understand the void so that we can more effectively address it? As pointed out above, there are three sources to the void.

The three sources of the void are the Three Misalignments. When we have unhealthy reactions to the three misalignments, we empower the Dark, Negative Attitude until it dominates our self-concept. The first misalignment is between expectations and reality.

Expectations and Realities

Cognitive psychologist Daniel Gilbert calls the brain an "anticipation machine." Our ability to use past experiences and current information to predict the future allows us to behave so as to increase the odds of our desired outcomes. Our ability to achieve these outcomes is directly related to our foresight, or our certainty regarding future events—how likely they are, when they will occur, and what they will be like.

When we are uncertainty about a possible future threat we will struggle to avoid its negative impact, and thus we will become anxious. Sometimes, this anxiety can lead us to adopt maladaptive strategies that make things worse.

Anxiety about the future isn't always negative. Positive anxiety occurs when we feel anticipation for something good to come. It's the butterflies in your stomach when you start the first day of high school and you can't wait to meet new friends and try new activities. It's the euphoric feeling of getting a promising new job with corporate perks, bigger paychecks, and talented coworkers. Your first week in the office can feel like floating on cloud nine as you anticipate what a great gig it will be. Positive anxiety is what makes your heart sing after a great date at the start of a new romantic relationship, as your mind surges with visions of wonderful dates to come.

There is a caveat to this excitement, though. While positive anxiety might feel better than negative anxiety, it's still based on anticipating a future that isn't reality. That excitement about the new job is an illusion. As soon as you learn that your coworkers are a nightmare to deal with, you can either accept reality and return to the Track of Humility, or you can pretend they're top brass to maintain your illusion of an amazing new job. This distortion of reality can lead you astray by causing you to ignore more red flags about your new job and stay in an unfulfilling position for too long.

And then there is the more familiar feeling of negative anxiety. You experience this when you are afraid that something horrible might happen. The end of senior year is bittersweet. You are excited about your new life but you also fear that you will never be as close with your high school friends again. When you put in your two-week's notice at the end of a job, you feel like a dead man walking. Your coworkers brush you off because you're on your way out, and you're not sure that your next job will be better, so you start to doubt whether leaving is the right choice at all. When you want to get out of a relationship, you dread the breakup. As you work up the nerve to say something you stop putting in the effort to enjoy spending time with your significant other.

Both positive and negative anxiety create a misalignment between expectations and reality, which can lead to a self-fulfilling cycle. One unfortunate example comes from a colleague of mine who feared his girlfriend would leave him, so he began to dread a future breakup. He was uncertain about their future together and started to pull away. This maladaptive coping strategy caused his girlfriend to change her behavior. She hadn't been thinking about leaving him at all—but now she was. She thought my colleague's distance indicated he was interested in other girls. When she felt replaceable, she sought a man who would better appreciate her. So she cheated. My colleague experienced a disconnect between his expectations and what was actually going on, so he distorted reality until it lined up. He acted like a breakup was imminent, even though neither party wanted that, and he caused it to occur.

In some situations anxiety can certainly be a useful tool to help you evaluate threats. If you get anxious when the bouncer outside the bar keeps brandishing his knife, it might motivate you to find a different bar. While you can't predict whether he'll get rough with someone, you can listen to your anxiety, and that could save you from a new scar. However, it also could prevent you from meeting your future wife sitting alone at the bar waiting for Mr. Right to walk in. In this case, your fear has distorted your reality so you never met your dream girl.

Positive anxiety can be exhilarating. Betting your whole paycheck on the black numbers of the roulette table is an exciting form of uncertainty. *If I win, I'll take my girl out for steaks and wine and still have some money leftover.* But when the ceramic ball lands on red and your rent money disappears before your eyes, a negative form of anxiety takes over. *How am I going to explain this one…* What inspired you to place this unwise bet in the first place? You distorted reality to convince yourself you had a good chance of winning, so you bet it all. When you lost the game and saw that reality didn't line up with your expectations, your anxiety flipped from positive to negative and you became dissatisfied.

Any form of anxiety, positive or negative, can lead to crippling distortions; the broken shards of glass in our mirror. This is because the brain wants to anticipate the future, even when it doesn't have enough information to do so. When you begin to take actions based on your predictions and discover a gap between your expected outcomes and reality you'll move from positive anxiety to negative.

Any space between our mental vision of the future and the truth of the present moment creates an uncomfortable misalignment. To fill this void, we distort our futures, our abilities, and our impressions to try and force alignment. This can reduce anxiety and protect your ego from admitting shortcomings when you experience expectation-reality misalignment. As a result, though, you'll fall off the Track of Humility and into the traps.

All Anxieties Have Draw-Backs

When you start a relationship you might develop positive anxiety and create imaginary certainties out of an uncertain situation. For example, you might fall head-over-heels and start planning your future kids' names by the second date. *I'm so excited for what's to come, we're going to be together forever.* This is a distorted view of the future that sets expectations too high, leading you into the Grandiose Mindset.

Next you might think, *This time will be different even though I had ten bad dates with ten bad people this month. It's not my fault those dates didn't work out. I just didn't meet anyone suitable for me.* This is a distortion of your self-concept that protects you from facing your inadequacies. Furthermore, you might imagine those "bad" dates not as failures, but as successes because you didn't get roped into a relationship below your standards. This attitude will propel you into the Entitlement Mindset.

You could further reason, *I'm just astronomically unlucky that I keep getting blind-sided by all these atrocious people. They're the real reason why it's not working out.* This is a distortion of your impressions about others. After briefly falling into despair that your last dozen dates didn't work out, you quickly deflect responsibility, blame it on everyone else, and enter the Excuses Mindset.

These three distortions are attempts to warp reality so it fits your expectations. You maintain these illusions because you don't want to experience a loss. They all stem from the Dark, Negative Attitude, which pushes you to try and fill the void instead of understanding it.

The same distortions can occur when you experience negative anxiety at the end of a relationship. It's easy to feel fatalistic after a breakup and supplement a fear of the unknown with a certainty such as *I'll never find love again, this was my last chance and I'll be depressed forever.* This distorted look at the future throws you straight into the Despair Mindset. You might pity yourself with cognitions of, *I'm too old, ugly, and poor to start dating anyone.* By entertaining those thoughts, you ignore counter evidence, which either keeps you in a Despair Mindset or launches you further off the Track of Humility into the Discreditable Mindset. Alternatively, you might also think, *There's no one out there who will appreciate a person like me. All they want is a young, attractive, rich person.* This distortion about others is not founded in reality and pushes you into the Excuses Mindset.

Both positive and negative anxiety feed the Dark, Negative Attitude and lead to an unhealthy mindset. To cope with feelings of positive and negative anxiety, you might accept, deflect, or fight them. Accepting anxieties by giving up and reasoning the problem is out of your control takes you off the Band of the Humility and into unhealthy mindsets like Entitlement or Excuses. Deflecting the problem by ignoring it or refuting contrary evidence leads you to the Charlatan and Discreditable Mindsets. Fighting the problem by lashing out traps you in the Grandiose, Entitlement, and Charlatan Mindsets. However, none of these unhealthy reactions to misalignment will help you understand the void. These approaches are all based on filling the void, but that won't change the dissatisfaction, disconnection, and impending doom you feel when you experience an expectation-reality misalignment.

You might have noticed that deflection, arrogance, and finger pointing are common themes when it comes to filling the void. This is due to loss aversion theory, self-concept protection, and the fundamental attribution error: *their fault, not mine.* As we saw in Chapter 1, people tend to attribute negative experiences to outside influences rather than to themselves. That's why it's common to ameliorate anxiety by underplaying our personal responsibility when we encounter an expectation-reality misalignment.

Our brains are anticipation machines. When our expectations don't match reality, it's natural to wonder why. We create questions and theories to distort our realities, but these distortions reinforce the Dark, Negative Attitude. And this attitude encourages us to maintain our distortions. It's a vicious cycle, and one that we often cannot break free of on our own.

Will you cope with unpredictability, dissatisfaction, and anxiety through an unhealthy mindset, or will you carve a different path? The alternative approach is to understand the void, which you can accomplish by building a strong team of people in your corner. I'll tell you how after we examine the next two misalignments.

Wants and Goals

Do you have an end of year goal or a New Year's resolution? Studies show that about 77 percent of us keep our New Year's resolutions past the first week—sadly, only about 19 percent of us achieve success after two years.

We all want things, but for some reason, even our simplest goals can go unattained. Among Americans who make New Year's resolutions, an online survey suggests the most common goals are exercising more (50%), saving money (49%), eating more healthily (43%), and losing weight (37%). These don't sound particularly challenging. You'd be able to knock most of them out at once if you simply cooked healthy meals at home instead of going out for burgers and beers on the weekends. A small life adjustment like this seems relatively easy, so why do New Year's resolutions have such a low success rate?

Our wants and our goals aren't the same thing. Wants occur in the present and goals exist in the future. If we want to eat healthier, we will start eating healthier. We're happy to do it, have intrinsic motivation, and we're probably doing it already. In this scenario, our want to eat healthy happens presently. Our future goal to eat healthier is actively being accomplished by our present daily actions. Thus, our wants and goals are in perfect alignment and we experience happiness and satisfaction.

If our goal is to eat healthier in the future, but we don't really want to substitute the carbs for fiber in the present, we are experiencing a wants/goals mismatch. There is a fundamental misalignment here. We wish we wantedto eat healthier, but we'd really rather stick to chips and guac. Wanting is a present reality, wishing we wanted is a distant desire. When our wants and goals are misaligned, it leaves us in a perpetual state of not getting what we think we want. We're disappointed in what we have, beat ourselves up, and base our happiness on external measures of success, such as keeping up with the Joneses.

The discomfort we experience from misaligned wants and goals can be explained using a concept from motivation psychology. Motivation is said to have both internal and external components. Internal motivation is when we engage in a behavior because we find it naturally gratifying. When we are internally motivated we will do something primarily for its own sake rather than for an external reward. The behavior itself validates our internal desires. True wants are internally motivated. They are things we naturally desire to do.

External motivation is when we do something to earn a reward or avoid punishment. When we are motivated by external forces we engage in activity not because we enjoy it or because we find it satisfying, but because we expect to get something in return or to avoid something unpleasant. Our goals and New Year's resolutions fall into this category. We wish we wanted them, but we don't.

When we chow down the eggplant and broccoli casserole for the third day in a row while making hungry eyes at our neighbor's steak and wine dinner, we're doing it for one of two reasons. It could be that we want the reward of being thinner or more vibrant. We might want the social approval of committing to a diet. However, we don't really want to eat the casserole. We wish we wanted to eat it. But we don't. This misalignment of wants and goals creates unhappiness and dissatisfaction. In this example, our goal is to satisfy third party influences.

A second reason for persisting with such a diet, though, might be a deep desire to provide our body with the very best nutrients possible, because we want to prolong and enhance the quality of our life. In this case we really want to eat the casserole, so our goals and wants are in alignment.

The reason we don't hold onto our New Year's resolutions is because they are often externally motivated. If we truly wanted to do them, we would have started them in December. Scientific research backs up. In fact, the best-known model for creativity and innovation in the workplace by Amabile (1988) holds that internal motivation leads to better workplace outcomes. Employees who feel their work is rewarding achieve greater innovative goals than those who are driven by promotions and bonuses. External motivation simply does not feel as good as internal motivation, so when we are responding to external motivation we tend to give up or fall short on our goals.

You might think a combination of internal and external motivators would yield the best outcomes, but shockingly, external motivations can take away from internal motivations through a phenomenon called the overjustification effect. A 1988 study demonstrates that children who were rewarded for playing with a toy became less interested in playing with it. When your wants feel externally motivated, pursuing them becomes less satisfying.

External motivation can be helpful in some cases because it's an effective way to motivate yourself to do something you don't want to do. If you dread doing your taxes, you might consider the punishment of failing to file on time to get yourself moving. Alternatively, you could promise yourself a reward to motivate yourself to file, such as taking a vacation once your paperwork is squared away with the IRS. However, both instances aren't truly rewarding. They don't encourage you to *want* to do your taxes. They are forms of wishing you wanted to do them. You'll still grit your teeth through the whole process, hating every minute of it. Is that any way to live?

If my goal was to do my taxes but I didn't want to do them, I would hire an accountant. Distorting our goals and wants into alignment with each other when they aren't really aligned won't make us happier or more satisfied. When our external wants are misaligned with our internal wants, we become unhappy and dissatisfied. Instead of understanding the void, many of us choose to fill it instead.

For a better picture of how wants and goals function, we can think about a pilot light underneath a furnace. When the temperature drops, the thermostat sends a signal to the furnace to heat up. The coldness creates a desire for heat. Once the furnace has brought the temperature back to the desired warmth, the switch on the thermostat goes off. But the pilot light remains on.

When a person is smoking a cigarette, the pilot light is their internal craving for a smoke. As long as the pilot light remains lit, they will always be a smoker, even if they claim they want to quit. Having a cigarette might satisfy their craving for a while, just as heating the room turns off the furnace. But the pilot light never goes out.

The goal of this book is to find out what's truly fueling your pilot light and discover how to cut off its fuel supply. That way, the next time the temperature drops, and your craving demands to be met, there will be no pilot light to stoke up the fire.

Let's take a look at an example of a smoker who wishes she wanted to quit smoking, but at the same time truly wants to continue.

Want to Quit Smoking?

Marla has been smoking cigarettes since she was fourteen years old. Her mom smokes, her brother smokes, and all of her friends smoke. Now 25, she's living with friends in the city, going out to bars, and smoking a lot. One day she decides to put down the pack for good. *No more smoking for me*, she thinks to herself. This decision lasts about one week.

There are tools available to Marla to help her quit smoking. She could use a smoke-free nicotine substitute like a vaporizer, chewing gum, or "the patch" to help taper off the addictive drug. She could go to addiction counseling or support groups. She could invest her time in meditation, exercise, or tracking the money she's saving as a nonsmoker. But she doesn't want to.

After purchasing her third "quitting pack" of the week, Marla is starting to feel ashamed. She wants to quit, but she also loves smoking. It's not just the addictive nature of the substance. She's been able to put down alcohol, cocaine, and marijuana without a second thought. There's something different about her relationship with cigarettes. *I'll never be able to quit. I'm a failure,* she tells herself.

Marla's problem is that her pilot light remains fueled. Her cravings for alcohol, cocaine, and marijuana didn't disappear, but went into fueling the pilot light that now burns only for cigarettes. Smoking is her hardest habit to crack not because nicotine is the most addictive, but because it is the only remaining habit that can relieve the energy from that pilot light. Like a warming furnace, she has to do something when the temperature drops. Marla cannot hope to stop smoking until she comes to an understanding of what is fueling her pilot light and what is causing her temperature to drop, and if she doesn't want to do that her wants and her goals will remain misaligned.

This is when our core self-worth and self-respect are revealed. Are we willing to do the work to discover what is actually going on inside of us? We may not know what life will look like on the other side of our discovery, but do we have faith that our quality of life will be better once we get there?

Marla enjoys smoking cigarettes, but her idea of a better life is smoke-free.

She can never be satisfied with this ongoing cognitive dissonance. She's either missing out on her favorite fix or missing out on the life she dreams about. This is the misalignment of wants and goals. She doesn't want the furnace of her addiction to start up again, but she's unwilling to address her pilot light or find other ways to keep the temperature up. She starts to hate herself and falls into despair because she can't seem to act in the ways she wishes she could.

While going smoke-free is a healthier choice and I don't recommend smoking cigarettes, I also don't recommend someone like Marla bending over backwards to do something she doesn't want to do. She's well-aware of the consequences of smoking. She's not trying to hook others on smoking. It's her independent choice to smoke because she's not ready to quit. For now, the perceived benefits of the warm furnace outweigh the perceived risks of cutting off the pilot light's fuel source. Enjoyment outweighs the struggle to put cigarettes down.

If Marla truly wanted to quit smoking, then laying off the cigarettes would be a positive experience. She would feel better every day she didn't smoke. She would be proud of herself for accomplishing what she set out to do and revel in the benefits of saving money, breathing easier, and having more energy. The decision would be from within, and not from social pressure like her friends' guilt trips. Quitting would still be hard, but the experience would be rewarding instead of punishing.

On the other hand, Marla's false wanting produces negative internal rhetoric and misaligns with her true desire to continue smoking. This creates a void that summons the Dark, Negative Attitude. Marla pities herself because she "wants" to quit, but believes she's too pathetic to maintain a smoke-free lifestyle. Filling the void with the Dark, Negative Attitude encourages her to deflect responsibility and say, "It's not my fault I'm addicted. I'm a victim. I can't do it myself no matter how hard I try."

Clearly the misalignment between wants and goals can lead to traps like the Despair, Excuses, and Discreditable Mindsets. Trying to achieve goals you don't truly want to achieve won't get you far and you'll set yourself up for disappointment. Without carefully hand-selected people in your corner to guide you, it's nearly impossible to see what's fueling your pilot light and get your wants and goals in alignment.

To understand the void instead of filling it we must avoid excuses, be honest with ourselves, and take responsibility.

Our pilot light ignites the flames of our bad habits, which takes us off track from accomplishing what we see as truly valuable. We know that at our core we all want our cravings fulfilled, but we wish we didn't want it. We can't stop the cycle until we find the strength within ourselves through sheer will and discipline to cut off that unconscious fuel source.

When Marla truly wants to quit, she'll be able to. She just doesn't want to right now, she only wishes she did.

And remember, if you wanted to keep your New Year's resolution, you'd have already started it last year.

Values and Behaviors

The third and final misalignment occurs when our behavior doesn't match what we know is right. There are universal ethics, or values systems, that all of us understand, even when our behavior doesn't reflect them. A wide body of research suggests there are a few invariable morals that are universal among humans.

In 1906, a monumental, but now antiquated, ethnographic survey from Finnish philosopher Edvard Westermarck revealed that the folklore in every culture he studied prohibited homicide and theft. The same survey noted the universal approval of charity, generosity, mutual aid, and honesty. While Westermarck only surveyed European and African traditions, his analysis provided a backbone for future moral universalist research.

More recent studies from O'Neill & Petrinovich (1998), Henrich et al. (2005), and Hauser, et al. (2007) converge on two commonalities that persist throughout all humanity: Human beings prefer to help the greater amount of people between two groups, and to treat each other with fairness. These values are not affected by elitism, social contracts, or cultural background. To boil down these findings into an often-repeated golden rule: We want to treat others how we wish to be treated.

These ethics are black and white. Humans instinctively know the difference between right and wrong. However, we don't always do what's right. Often our behaviors aren't in alignment with our values. When our actions and morals are misaligned, we experience uncomfortable cognitive dissonance and seek to fill the void.

Even sociopaths and serial killers, who don't appear to regret their crimes against humanity, still know their actions are misaligned with morality. They know what they're doing is perceived by others as wrong, or else they wouldn't try so hard to cover their tracks. They'd attack people in broad daylight if they thought they had the moral high ground. But they don't. And I can guarantee they don't want strangers to treat them the same way they treat their victims.

You could say the same about gang members or mafiosos. They create their own moral code that allows them to commit crimes with good justification, such as *I'm killing for my family. I'm righting an injustice. I'm doing this in the name of God.* But even these people don't really experience an alignment of values and behaviors. Their moral code is a distortion. When a mafia soldier kills for the first time, they feel awful. They vomit while their associates grab them a drink to numb the pain. Then they go to church and ask for forgiveness. Did I mention they're wearing crosses around their necks the whole time? Murderers know that killing is wrong and use a variety of tricks to quell their cognitive dissonance and distort their values until their crimes appear morally acceptable.

I hope most of you readers are not sociopaths or murderers, so let's use a more down-to-earth example: lying.

In 1957, Leon Festinger devised the most boring task imaginable to test what would happen if he paid people to tell a lie. The task was simple: turn pegs for an indeterminate amount of time. He pretended the point of the task was to gauge motor skills, but the real test happened after participants left the peg board.

That's when Festinger asked the subjects to lie to the next "participant" (a disguised researcher) about how fun the task was. Festinger would say something like, "Our guy who usually tells the subjects how fun the experiment is happens to be out sick today. Can you fill in? We'll compensate you for your time. Just go out there and convince the next subject that this experiment is a hoot."

The peg-turning task was designed to be as boring as possible. No one thought it was fun in earnest. However, some subjects started to reevaluate their appraisal after telling the next "participant" how great the task would be. A conversation might go something like this:

"I'm telling you man, this experiment is the bees' knees. It'll really knock your socks off. It might seem a little strange at first, but once you get into it you'll feel great."

"Really? Because a friend of mine was in this study last week and he felt the complete opposite. He didn't have a good time at all. He even warned me, 'whatever you do, don't do that task. It's the most boring thing I've ever done.'"

"No, no, your friend has it all wrong. I swear, this experiment is very fun. One of the best experiments out there."

When he gave them their compensation, Festinger paid some subjects $1 for telling the lie while he paid other $20. Then he asked them to honestly tell him what they thought of the boring task. The $20 people admitted they hated it while the $1 people kept pretending they really enjoyed it. How come?

Here's what happened. Those who were paid $20 could use the cash to justify their lies. On the other hand, the ones who were paid $1 could not justify their lies with the meager payment. Instead, their values were called into check. The subjects paid $1 were personally invested in the lie, so they distorted their behavior and convinced themselves the experiment *was* fun to reduce their cognitive dissonance and align their behaviors with their values.

Lying is universally immoral because it is not fair and nobody wants to be lied to. The subjects knew that lying was wrong. They were uncomfortable because they experienced a misalignment between their behaviors and values. To fill the void and protect their self-image, they left the experiment convinced that the peg-turning task was truly fun. They chose to protect their ego and maintain the distortion.

Filling the void when our behaviors and values misalign provokes the Dark, Negative Attitude. Without proper accountability, we lie to ourselves and others to keep cognitive dissonance at bay. We get defensive when our character is called into question. We operate with deceit and dishonesty to hide our wrongdoings. We become invested in building grand illusions and won't admit our mistakes. This is a slippery slope that can whisk us off the Track of Humility very quickly.

The good news about these distortions is that we actually know better, and with some humility we can bring ourselves back into alignment. We lie when we behave in ways that we know are wrong. Find the self-worth within yourself to live parallel to your value system.

Our behaviors may vary but our values don't. When we start to get uncomfortable because we experience a misalignment, it's easy to use the Dark, Negative attitude to fill the void. However, understanding the void can get us back on the Track of Humility. It takes a lot of courage to admit that you're not acting in accordance with your values, but if you can pull it off, it might save your life...

Flying with the Lights On

On the Day the Music Died, the pilot, Roger Peterson, experienced misalignment when he expected he could fly in low visibility conditions despite lacking the required field training. He figured he could weather the storm and perhaps prove himself as a competent pilot. There was no one present to make him aware of his disillusionment. He filled the void with the Grandiose Mindset and flew for the last time.

Buddy Holly misaligned his wants and goals throughout his experience of the "Tour from Hell." He didn't really want his friends to freeze half to death. He didn't want to lose sleep and become delirious. And he wished he wanted to see the tour to the end no matter what so he could make enough money for his family. He filled the void with the Entitlement Mindset and never saw his family again.

The tour managers with General Artists Corporation misaligned their behaviors with their values. They disregarded the intensity of the grueling Winter Dance Party tour because they cared more about money than the well being of others. They never would have put themselves through such misery, but they subjected the musicians to it despite their protests. Ultimately, these record executives distorted their reality enough to claim, *We're the managers, we're doing the right thing, we have it all figured out,* even though their scheduling was nonsensical and harsh. They filled the void with the Charlatan Mindset and influenced the musicians to make their own travel plans as a last ditch effort.

Reacting to challenging circumstances with the valued input of other people would have prevented this tragedy. Unfortunately, all decisions were made in the void, and the Dark, Negative Attitude won out.

Our own distorted desires to fill the void destroy our potential for gaining powerful foresight. Trying to fill the void only bolsters an unhealthy mindset of inadequacy, which can generate feelings of envy, jealousy, and dissatisfaction. It leads us off the Track of Humility and into ruin.

If you think you can make it through the checkpoints all by yourself, you are still filling the void instead of understanding it. To understand the void is to acknowledge that you cannot walk this path alone. It's an illusion to think you're only in a rough patch temporarily, but given enough time the stars will align and bring you back to the Track of Humility. How do you think you got trapped in the first place? You are (or were) in the Grandiose Mindset if you think you can figure out your biases and inadequacies without help from the right people in your corner.

There is a solution to this problem and it requires taking responsibility, asking for help, and operating with a team of qualified individuals. It's not about making "better" choices, it's about making different choices. And in order to consider different choices, we must listen to a variety of voices. When we do, we gain clarity on the choices that exist.

When discussing your choices with a trusted advisor, do the best you can to share your version of the story honestly and accurately. Most people change the narrative subtly to influence their advisor to say what they want to hear. When you manipulate the facts you will inadvertently manipulate your advisor to reinforce the mindset that got you into trouble in the first place. When you are honest and accurate in your discussion, you will find yourself presented with three primary categories of alternative choices.

The first choice is to stop fixating on the future. When you set your expectations far in the future, you're begging for anxiety and misalignment. Instead, work with the people in your corner to keep your expectations grounded in reality. When we operate this way with our team, we cultivate respect, imagination, and efficiency. We experience gratitude for what we have, but also inspiration to ask for more. We look upon the Joneses with admiration instead of envy.

The second choice is to identify your true strengths and weaknesses so you can make healthy evaluations and develop an internal source of motivation. Without an internal source of motivation you'll find your goals won't align with your core wants (your pilot light). A team of people in your corner can keep your wants and goals aligned by guiding you to look inward and improve rather than seeking approval from outside sources or tearing yourself down for your inadequacies. They can encourage you to go out and accomplish something you truly want.

The third choice is to look yourself in the mirror and critically evaluate whether your behaviors are in line with your values. Are you doing the right things for the right reasons in the right ways? A team that is clear on these values can hold you accountable and can provide alternative perspectives to help you understand your past decisions and the motivations behind them. This way you can stop forcing alignment and distorting reality. With the right team of people in your corner you can honestly examine whether your behaviors align with a value system of honesty, self-awareness, and integrity. You can search for inconsistencies and misalignments between how you feel and what you do. This way, you can make the necessary improvements.

Developing a trustworthy team of people in your corner can help guard against the Dark, Negative Attitude. As a result, you will better serve yourself and the people around you. You will yield healthy, solid, confident relationships. You will feel accomplishment for your successes. And most importantly, you won't look into a shattered mirror and squint to see yourself as whole. With help you will fix the mirror. Then you will grow to appreciate and respect the person who's looking back at you.

Over the rest of this book I'll help you figure out how to accomplish all of this. I'll unveil the strategies to organize this incredible team of people in your corner in Chapter 4…

Chapter 4
Blindspots

The Cabinet of Rivals

The election of 1861 would decide who would bear the onus of leading America through a civil war. Would it be veteran Missouri statesman, Edward Bates? Ohio governor, Chase? Perhaps the experienced New York senator, William H. Seward? Certainly it wouldn't be that rookie in the top hat they called Honest Abe.

It didn't seem like he had a chance, but on March 4, Abraham Lincoln took the oath of office and became the sixteenth President of the United States. Lincoln had earned a reputation for being a fair man during his career as a lawyer, but his knowledge of politics was meager compared to his competitors for the Republican ticket. Yet, he was tasked with one of the most daunting challenges in American political history.

Uniting the tumultuous nation wouldn't be possible until he looked himself in the mirror and unflinchingly embraced his potential weaknesses. He understood he had blindspots in his political experience and needed to find some way to cover them. To lead the nation during the looming crisis, Lincoln appointed a group of opinionated, stubborn, and powerful secretaries. They weren't his friends, they were his adversaries. Lincoln's famous cabinet, which became known as his "team of rivals," demonstrates how having the right people in your corner can keep you on the Track of Humility so you can achieve your goals.

To repair the Union, Lincoln knew he would have to strengthen tenuous bonds between the various factions remaining in the North. However, he didn't have the long career nor the personal ties to earn the respect of each Union associate party. He also knew the Republican Party was in its infancy and its members came from a variety of different political backgrounds like Whigs and Democrats.

By recognizing these blindspots, Lincoln figured he could use his cabinet appointments to offer strategic coalitions across the country. First, Lincoln selected former Republican Party rivals for three of the most important cabinet positions: Senator William H. Seward became the Secretary of State, Ohio governor Salmon P. Chase became Secretary of the Treasury, and Edward Bates of Missouri became the Attorney General.

Next, Lincoln appointed former Democrats to build bipartisan support: Secretary of the Navy Gideon Welles, Postmaster General Montgomery Blair, and Secretary of War Edwin Stanton. These appointments also extended representation to crucial states from the northeast, old northwest, and border states. By putting his rivals in his cabinet, Lincoln gained access to a wide range of opinions, which he realized would sharpen his own thinking. It also gave him a way of keeping many conflicting groups working together. If he didn't have a unified nation fighting against the South, the fight would be impossible to sustain. This provided maximum coverage over his geographic blindspots throughout the nation as well as his blindspots in political experience. Bringing together those conflicting opinions in his cabinet not only helped Lincoln; it helped the country as well.

In this wood engraving from Frank Leslie's Illustrated Newspaper, February 2, 1861, President-elect Lincoln is shown using Union glue to repair a split cabinet, which represents the divide between North and South.

All six of his appointed cabinet members were more educated, better known, and had more government experience than Lincoln himself. They came from privileged backgrounds and had attended fine colleges, while Lincoln was not college-educated and taught himself everything, including law. It would have been easy for Lincoln to appoint officials with similar or lesser experience than he had, or to surround himself with Yes-Men who would agree no matter what. However, this would only serve Lincoln's ego and not the divided nation. Lincoln avoided a Grandiose Mindset and sought out his staunchest opponents because he needed qualifications, credibility, and experience. Not cheerleaders.

At the beginning, Lincoln's secretaries were barely on speaking terms with each other. They had strong, conflicting personalities and only communicated when necessary. However, Lincoln skillfully used their strengths to increase his foresight and support the Union cause.

Lincoln was so focused on maximizing his foresight he made sure all aspects of his life were aligned with achieving his goal. His primary workspace was a mahogany desk free from clutter, organized with only the most important papers, and home to the most relevant color-coded map used to track Union generals and armies. His office was strewn with maps of advancing troops, which he updated daily. He referred to the office as "the shop" and always left the door open to his three secretaries so he could hear a variety of opinions and ideas that would help him shape the next move.

Much like the worn furnishings in the room, Lincoln frequently dressed in clothes that had seen better days. He wore a baggy black suit, which hung loosely on his tall, wiry frame. He had holes in his socks from pacing the room without slippers during every meeting. He greeted dignitaries in faded old coats because building healthy relationships took precedence over looking like a million bucks.

The meeting space and culture reveals much about Lincoln's leadership. Lincoln never strayed too far from the Track of Humility. He didn't let pride, arrogance, or envy cloud his judgements or foresight. He didn't operate with the Dark, Negative energy and try to fill any voids in his life, but sought to understand the voids and bring the right people into his corner to cover his blindspots. He didn't overshoot his expectations or ignore contrary evidence and opinions. He embraced healthy conflict, celebrating the strengths of others while understanding his own weaknesses. For example, Lincoln didn't know as much about financial matters, so he generally trusted Seward's decades of experience to handle diplomacy. He selected individuals he admired, trusted, and could rely on for their expertise and advice.

Lincoln understood that healthy relationships are at the core of productivity, and that if you deal with people in the right manner then you will have no problem working effectively with them. When something went well, Lincoln always shared the credit. When something went wrong, he shouldered his share of the blame. When he made a mistake, he acknowledged it immediately. He treated his cabinet members respectfully and fairly. He behaved in a way that aligned with his beliefs about being a good teammate. He operated with the Bright, Positive Attitude.

Although he reserved final decision making power for himself, Lincoln involved his secretaries closely in his decision-making process. He consulted them as a group when contemplating major military decisions. The cabinet played a crucial role in many of Lincoln's most notable moments as president, from the decision to surrender Fort Sumter and Pickens without a fight in

1861, to the Emancipation Proclamation, to the final campaign that led to Confederate Leader Robert E. Lee's surrender at Appomattox.

Lincoln's successes required an enormous amount of humility. We all have blindspots and misalignments in our lives that we want to compensate for. It's easy to attempt to hide them instead of seeking to understand them. If we operate with the Dark, Negative Attitude, we might try to fill the voids with distortions and fall off the Track of Humility. It's natural to want to ignore our own blindspots to protect our ego, but that will inhibit our foresight and we will end up falling into the traps. Luckily, we can deal with our blindspots in a healthier way.

If we admit we need help bringing our life into alignment we can get the right people in our corner to make sure we stay on the Track of Humility. We aren't always aware of our blindspots, so the expertise and honesty of trusted advisors can help us see what areas of our lives we need to work on in order to be successful.

Locating your Blindspots

To assemble the best team of advisors, we first need to identify our major blindspots. Some are quite obvious, while others are more subtle. This means taking a good, hard look at ourselves. Practicing generosity, honor, self-respect, and the respect of others begins with a daily reflection in the mirror. We must consider where our ego might be unconsciously filling in some character gaps. Take the following example:

You can test your literal blind spot by looking at the images below.

+   •

Look at the plus sign and the circle. Position your nose somewhere between them.

Close your left eye, and focus on the plus sign with your right eye. Do not look deliberately at the circle.

Now move closer to the page, gradually. Don't take your focus off the plus sign.

At some point around one foot away from the page, the circle will disappear from your peripheral vision. Your brain will use the surrounding color to fill in the empty space.

That is your literal blind spot.

This simple test demonstrates how we can have blindspots we aren't aware of until we put them to the test. We all have blindspots in our visual field at all times because they represent an area of our eyeball with no rods or cones to detect light.

Instead of seeing an uncomfortable blindspot in our vision all day long, we use our brain to fill in the gap for us. We don't like uncertainties or anomalies so we create a distortion to compensate. But this phenomenon isn't limited to a specific area in our visual field. Our brains also blind us from seeing dynamic, moving objects right in front of our eyes, like the invisible gorilla study we saw in the Introduction.

This experiment reveals two things: we are missing a lot of what goes on around us, and we have no idea that we are missing so much. We can't have proper foresight if we only see a portion of what's in front of us. Therefore, we must find a way to compensate for our blindspots using trusted advisors in our lives.

We can find our blindspots using methods similar to the plus and circle test. We can run a routine test of every aspect of our lives, searching for weaknesses like we gradually move our head further from the page until we notice our blindspot. This is possible through daily reflection and quality self-criticism, but it's not the most accurate way to uncover your blindspots and increase your foresight.

The Dunning-Krueger effect demonstrates that we tend to underestimate our areas of inadequacy, so there could be gorilla-sizes holes in our lives that we don't recognize as weaknesses. Further, the 20% rule states that our blindspots get larger the more invested we become in anything. We simply cannot always see our biases and deficiencies. These effects can challenge us at the three checkpoints, pulling us into traps such as Grandiosity or Discreditability. This is why we shouldn't completely rely on ourselves to stay on the Track of

Humility. We all need a little help from the people in our corner to avoid diving headfirst into situations we're not ready for.

What Lincoln did was unprecedented at that time. No one before him had thought to get people in their cabinet who disagreed with them. Lincoln was successful because he brought the right people into his corner to stay on the Track of Humility. It paid off for him and for America, establishing Lincoln as one of history's finest presidents.

While his secretaries initially resented Lincoln for his success, they grew to respect his decision-making skills. Bates even admitted that the president was "very near being a perfect man." In the end, these people came not only to respect Lincoln, but also to admire him. They grew together, becoming better and more accomplished politicians as a cohesive unit. The group of people who at first didn't speak to each other developed into colleagues that conversed prolifically through personal letters. Seward, who started as Lincoln's biggest rival, ultimately wrote to his wife, "The President is the best of us."

Getting the right people in our corner is the key to developing foresight. We all need the right people to help us see our blindspots and stay on the Track of Humility. You would be lucky to have more than five high-quality advisors in your corner, but five is more than enough. Being too lenient about who you let into your inner circle and trusting the wrong people could be disastrous. Think about what it could have meant if Lincoln left his office door open for ten strong personalities instead of his core three.

To assemble your presidential cabinet, you need to search for a few individuals who have good motives and good credentials. With these two qualities, the advisors in your corner will help you develop foresight and stay on the Track of Humility.

Evaluating Motives

When searching for someone to place in your corner, you must first evaluate motives. Good motives are crucial for advisors because with the right intentions they will be less likely to fall into traps that encourage them to distort reality and withhold their true feedback.

If someone's motives are in the wrong place, they're likely assisting you for the wrong reasons. They might aim to take advantage of your success after they've helped you. Or, maybe they are motivated by a tangible reward like an increased paycheck. These are bad motives because they can prevent your advisor from giving you honest feedback. If their true intention is not to help you they are not likely to give you honest feedback. And without that, your advisors won't be able to cover your blindspots or help you develop foresight.

Many close advisors prove to be interested in taking advantage of their colleagues. You don't want someone like Judas Iscariot in your corner. Judas was one of the Twelve Apostles of Jesus Christ. His responsibility was to manage the money being donated to Jesus' cause, but he is mostly known today for betraying Jesus to religious authorities in exchange for 30 pieces of silver. Jesus' other disciples would later discover that Judas had been embezzling funds from their cause. Judas' true intention was not to help Jesus, but to get rich quick.

Judas led religious authorities to Jesus while he was alone praying in a field and gave him the infamous "Judas Kiss" to identify him to the captors. Judas didn't have the same intentions as Jesus. He wasn't interested in spreading the Word of God. His intention was self-serving and he set Jesus up to be crucified.

Et tu, Brute?

This famous line of betrayal comes from William Shakespeare's *Julius Caesar*, in which Caesar's close political ally and friend, Brutus, stabs him to death. It's a fictional line that Caesar utters to his killer, in shock that his best friend would turn against him. This scene is based on the true story of Brutus, who was conflicted about joining the plot to kill the emperor, but was persuaded by other politicians. They led him to believe that killing Caesar would protect the future of Rome, so he stabbed Caesar to death instead of trying to reason with him. Brutus' intentions were to protect his own ego, so he caved to peer pressure instead of standing up for Caesar. In the end, he was not a good friend or advisor.

The Manhattan Project gathered some of the greatest scientific minds in the world to create an atomic bomb, but not everyone in this inner circle had the best intentions. Working closely together every day, the scientists had no idea that three of their colleagues—Theodore Hall, David Greenglass, and

Klaus Fuchs—were feeding their discoveries to the Soviets. Therefore the USSR detonated their first A-bomb in 1949, much earlier than the United States expected. The U.S. filled their corner with untrustworthy people and this may have inadvertently led to heightened nuclear tensions during the Cold War.

There is a way to filter out potential Judases and Brutuses from your corner. To quote Abraham Lincoln, "If you want to test a man's character, give him power."

Greed is tempting. Under a watchful eye, character can be unveiled when someone is given power or faced with an opportunity to seize power.

It's critical that you don't mistake friendliness for good intentions. Overly friendly people in your corner could be blowing smoke and inflating your ego instead of helping you see your blindspots. In this case, they might be trying to help or they might be buttering you up. They might have the right motives or the wrong motives. You need to watch them closely.

We are all susceptible to the same temptations. When faced with most common dilemmas, consider, what are you trying to accomplish, and what do you stand to gain? Realize that it is more valuable to solve an issue than to be "right."

Remember, there is a difference between being kind and being nice. Nice people tell you what you want to hear to avoid conflict, and they don't like to work against you, they would rather collaborate. Kind people are respectful of how you feel, and at the same time give you the truth regarding how they see the situation, no matter how much it may disappoint you in the short term.

This was likely the case with Justin Beiber's team, who didn't feel secure enough to tell Justin about one of his embarrassing blindspots. The teen pop star icon was getting ready to perform in front of thousands of fans, and he forgot to zip up his pants. Between his dressing room and the stage entrance, Beiber must have walked by at least thirty team members including wardrobe managers, agents, and friends. No one wanted to break it to the superstar that his fly was down. They wanted to stay on their boss's good side, not have an embarrassing conversation might make things awkward. Instead of watching out for Beiber's blindspots, they allowed him to walk into a social snafu as hundreds of open-zipper photos surfaced on the Internet.

The desire to be liked can be a horrible motivation for any relationship. This is why celebrities often date each other. If you are an attractive celebrity, you never know if the people you meet really care about you or if they are only in it for the money, attention, and glamor. Everyone you meet would put you on a pedestal and avoid getting into any type of conflict with you.

Celebrities could date people from just about any walk of life, from politicians and powerful executives, to grocery clerks and college students. Yet they often choose to date each other. They seem to believe that other celebrities might be less likely to become romantically involved for selfish purposes like getting rich. Celebrities already have fame and fortune and understand the burden of success. Therefore, they might be more honest about providing feedback and making a relationship healthy. Still, celebrities often draw up prenuptial contracts with each other because they can never be sure if their closest advisors, their fiancés, are totally pure of heart.

Clearly, having someone in your corner with the wrong motives is a deal-breaker. If the people in your corner are helping you for the wrong reasons, they might stab you in the back, take advantage of you, or inadvertently lead you astray. They will not prioritize your self-growth, and they could create new blindspots for you instead of covering old ones.

It's imperative that the people in your corner give you advice that serves you, not advice that hurts you. Without the right motives, your advisors will not increase your foresight. But what are the right motives?

The Right Stuff

To find someone with the right motives, look for signs of the Bright, Positive Attitude such as Light Triad personality traits. The Light Triad is a group of traits that are commonly found in the world's most well-reputable people. It serves as a reaction to research that identified the Dark Triad of personality types, which are associated with malicious people such as serial killers. Instead of focusing on the worst things about people, psychologist Scott Barry Kaufman proposed a Light Triad composed of Kantianism, Humanism, and Faith in Humanity. These three traits are a great place to start when deciding what it means to have the right motives. Let's break them down.

Kantianism means treating people as ends unto themselves, not as means. This means your advisors should derive a reward directly from assisting you, instead of using you as means to obtain another reward. You are the reward itself! People with Kantianism aren't operating from a place of envy, but from a place of genuine generosity. They will keep an eye out for your blindspots because they inherently enjoy doing it.

Humanism refers to valuing the character and dignity of each individual. If the people in your corner seem to respect their friends and enemies alike, that's a good sign they will treat all people like they have value. A Humanistic advisor is likely not going to act disrespectful or malicious because they understand that people don't deserve to be treated unfairly. If you have a Humanistic person in your corner, it's likely they won't operate from a place of judgment or hatred, so they will be able to stay on the Track of Humility. Further, if they value your worth as an individual instead of merely your accolades, they probably won't put you on a pedestal either. They will give you honest feedback on how to improve, rather than saying what they think will make you happy.

The third trait in the Light Triad is Faith in Humanity, which is about believing in the fundamental goodness of humans. Advisors with this quality are willing to help you grow instead writing you off as inadequate. They recognize that all people have deficiencies, and that this doesn't make us bad people. Rather than stabbing you to death because they fear you might make a poor political leader, they will figure out ways to cover your blindspots so you can be the best leader you can be.

Beyond the Light Triad, the most important thing to look for in an advisor is an alignment of motives. You want to make sure you and your advisors have goals that are mutual. These people should want you to succeed in the same way you want yourself to succeed. If an advisor's goals fall out of sync with yours, they will either have to leave your corner or they will betray you, like in the cases of the Manhattan Project and the Judas Kiss.

When the people in your corner have good motives, you will know their advice is intended to help you, not to hurt you. Instead of working for their own purposes, they will commit to covering your blindspots and helping you develop foresight. However, your advisors must also be effective communicators, which requires they have a thorough understanding of others through the art of empathic listening.

Be mindful of the truth of what you observe with regard to the motives of your potential advisors, and don't project your own desires onto them by assigning them traits they don't really possess. The decisions you have made in your past can affect your view of the future and cause you to see others as you wish they were, rather than as they truly are. In order to be fair to yourself and your potential advisors, you must approach these people with a clean slate and truly understand where they're coming from.

Discerning Someone's Motives

How can you be sure someone has good intentions before you try to recruit them to be one of your advisors? It can be hard to tell the difference between a person who helps you for the sake of building on the relationship versus one who helps for a reward. Make sure the people you select have a *vision beyond the moment*. To discern someone's intentions, ask them why they're willing to cover your blindspots. Are their intentions to build on the relationship and achieve an end result together, or are they using the relationship to get to their own end result?

One easy way to do this is to simply ask people what their goals are. Try to get an honest answer about why someone wants to advise you and make sure their goals line up with yours. If they honestly have different intentions than you, they probably aren't someone you want in your inner circle. Further, even if it sounds like they're telling you all the right things, you still have to be wary of deception. Three questions to keep in mind are:

- Does this person respect my time?
- Do they respect my health (physical or emotional)?
- Do they respect the boundaries of my privacy?

A good way to answer these three questions is to look at how a person treats everyone else. Don't fall into the illusion of thinking you are so special that people are going to treat you differently from how they treat everyone else. You're not. And they won't.

One way to judge whether someone is generally honest or tends to be deceptive is to observe how they react to fortune and misfortune. If they notice someone doing well, are they happy for that person or envious? Do they admire or despise them? And how does your potential advisor react when they experience fortune of their own? Do they congratulate themselves and brag or do they express humility and gratitude? Just as one can become intoxicated through substance abuse, one can also get high from success and sedated from failure. Substances, successes, and failures reveal the truth of one's character and underlying intentions. But I don't recommend getting potential advisors high to test their character.

One of the simplest ways to test someone's motives is to think about what they would do when a complete stranger trips on the stairs and drops paperwork everywhere. A person with good motives would stop and help that person purely for the joy of helping others. This is a demonstration of Kantianism. On the other hand, someone who passes by the stranger and insults them, laughs, or complains that they're in the way probably doesn't have good motives. They are more likely to see helping others as a means to an end instead of an end in itself.

Ultimately, you want to gauge two factors to determine whether a person has the right motives: Treating others right and treating themselves right. If an individual operates with the Bright, Positive Mindset in all aspects of their life and shares your goals, they probably will have the right intentions and cover your blindspots.

The best way to gauge these factors is to evaluate a potential advisor's reputation. According to the negativity bias, we remember bad news twice as intensely as we hold onto good news. This is why making a single mistake feels worse than doing two good deeds. We tend to place more emphasis on times when people hurt us or wronged us than on times when they were helpful and kind. For this reason, our reputation is twice as easy to mess up as it is to improve.

Establishing a long standing reputation of doing the right things for the right reasons is the best way a person can demonstrate that they will be good to you in the future. To evaluate reputation, ask others how they feel about a person. It doesn't have to be confrontational. Ask the question subtly with genuine curiosity.

If you want to evaluate a colleague ask others around the office what it was like working with her or how well they know her. If you express genuine curiosity, chances are good you'll be able to get reliable feedback about someone by surveying a handful of people who work closely with them. Keep in mind, your emotional state during your survey will determine whether you come across as an interrogator or as someone with genuine curiosity.

But be warned, you must take these judgments with a grain of salt. Everyone has biased opinions that might distort your opinion of an otherwise good candidate for your cabinet. Even Honest Abe had his enemies and detractors. Don't let one bad review rule someone out.

Look for general and long standing trends as evidence of good motives that line up with your goals. This way you can judge whether someone might be a good fit to put in your corner and increase your foresight.

Evaluating Credentials

Good intentions are the most important quality in a trusted advisor, but they aren't everything. As the saying goes, "the road to hell is paved with good intentions," meaning that even well-meaning people could lead you astray. After evaluating someone's motives, you should also evaluate their credentials.

Take the example of a phony tour guide. Imagine your friend invites you to an exotic island in the Pacific ocean because he wants to show you a good time. However, he's never been to this island before and doesn't know how it works. He might reassure you that it's going to be the best trip ever and that he'll look into all the details, but if he lacks experience with this new place, he might inadvertently lead you into tourist traps, bad parts of town, or other dangers. You wouldn't want him telling you which wild fruits were safe to eat and which were deadly. Or how to get a good deal on boat fare and avoid the vessels that might kidnap you. Even if all his intentions are in the right place, he might not see his own vulnerabilities and blindspots because he lacks the proper credentials.

You want someone who can guide you to a successful outcome and accurately notice your blindspots in their area of expertise. If one of your weaknesses is the inability to deal with clients and make them feel valuable, get a customer service master in your corner to coach you through it. If you're not great at scheduling enough down time with your family, find a trusted advisor who excels at balancing home and work life. Wherever you have blindspots, find someone who can respectfully hold you accountable and help you recognize problems you fail to notice or don't know much about. Part of blindspot coverage is having capable advisors with the right credentials to help you compensate for your shortcomings.

Credentials are so important to healthy collaboration that they are ranked as the number one reason for acceptance or rejection among hiring managers. The right experience and credibility makes or breaks a person's ability to excel in a role at a company. And for good reason, too. Many people try to fake their credentials and end up being problematic employees. They'll try to fool hiring managers with illegitimate stories and accolades to convince them they can offer something of value. They're as deep in the Charlatan Mindset as a snake oil salesman and will not be able to assess your blindspots because they won't know where to look. Don't let people with fake credentials like Mina Chang into your inner circle.

In November 2019, Mina Chang resigned from her senior State Department post after allegations of a phony resume and a photoshopped Time magazine cover. She claimed she was an alumna from Harvard who had also taken part in a UN panel about drones, and she also said she had led a successful program with US cadets at West Point. She constructed an entire fake lifestyle as a "humanitarian thought leader" through fake social media content.

The truth is that Mina only attended a short Harvard Business School course. And she had never worked with the UN, nor did she possess any expertise in drone technology. Her partnership with West Point was horribly flawed and promptly scrapped. Representatives from West Point had contacted her to remove their logo from her charity campaigns. She leveraged relationships with government officials to open doors and propped them open with fraudulent accolades. Had her fake credentials not come to light, Ms. Chang would possibly have worked within the US Agency for International Development overseeing the organization's work in Asia with a budget of one billion dollars. If it went anything like West Point, then substantial taxpayer dollars might have been squandered.

In another case from 2018, dozens of parents were charged as part of an admissions fraud scandal at schools such as Stanford, the University of Southern California, and the University of California in Los Angeles. In this scheme, parents had paid coaches to validate faked athletic credentials of their children including false roster information, statistics, and shots of the athlete "in action." Together with fudged SAT scores, the false athletic accolades could get these students admitted to prestigious schools under the guise of being top-tier athletes. Actor Lori Loughlin is one of the parents named by prosecutors to have paid officials to alter data and fraudulently admit her child as a student-athlete. You wouldn't want Lori Loughlin in your corner if she's willing to pay to get her kid to take an undeserved spot on the team in place of someone who actually earned it. Credentials are hard to earn, which is why they are so valuable when they are legitimate.

You want someone with good credentials to watch out for you because you know they won't try to pull the wool over your eyes. It's the same reason you wouldn't buy a product that was marketed with fake data. Take Power Balance for example. In their advertising, the company stated that Power Balance wristbands improved strength, balance, and flexibility. However the company later had to admit that there is no credible scientific evidence supporting their claims. They were compelled by law to publicly admit breaching Section 52 of the Trade Practices Act of 1974 and had to offer their customers full refunds. This example merely involves the misrepresentation of some minor effects from a plastic wristwatch, but imagine if your research or marketing guy tried to pass off fake data to you. Think of the implications of misrepresenting the capabilities of a life-saving medication. Or what if your rookie contractor misrepresented the amount of people who could safely stand on the second floor balcony he just installed? Without the proper credentials, you might have some lawsuits on your hands, like Power Balance.

In life and in businesses you always need to check someone's credentials before you let them into your corner. Otherwise, you might actually create more blindspots and lose foresight. This is a slippery slope to Grandiosity and unrealistic expectations because if you invest in unaccredited advice, it might be hard to admit you put blind faith in in the wrong person, leading you to double down on their advice even in the face of contrary evidence.

What Makes Someone Credible?

A credible person has experience. Not just a learners permit, or even a master's degree, but at least a decade of committed experience. Ten years of experience is a good ballpark to assess credibility because it means someone has been through ups and downs and figured out how to navigate a variety of situations.

When a company builds its Board of Directors, it doesn't include the startup team of twenty or thirty-something year olds. The Board is composed of industry veterans. Similarly, you want to look for advisors who have been through thick and thin and have achieved successful outcomes through successful processes. They can't be Charlatans. They need to have been around long enough to prove they actually know a thing or two about what it takes to get to the next level.

A credible person has successful processes. They aren't all talk and no walk. They can point to years of data demonstrating their successful processes, not just a few recent accolades that might be cherry-picked as an overrepresentation of their abilities.

This is why you wouldn't immediately invest your money with a broker who only has a few months of experience, even if during those few months the broker had good results. It's possible this person started investing during a period of economic growth, which makes it appear they made amazing financial choices. However, you have no way of assessing what sort of choices they would make during an economic downturn. If you had enough monkeys in a room throwing bananas at the stock ticker, at least one of them would make some incredible investment decisions by random chance. A small string of successes doesn't indicate that a person knows what they're doing. There are millions of individuals who are invested in the stock market, and if one of them becomes successful in a year, that doesn't mean you should give them your life savings. You need to look for a longer track record.

A credible person will also have a collection of accolades to back up their claims. While accolades are easy to fake, legitimate awards and certifications can add credibility to a person's track record. This shows dedication and mastery in a specific field, and praise from peers in that field. If you don't know much about real estate, but your agent has won some prestigious awards, has multiple business degrees from reputable schools, and is licensed to practice in multiple states, they might have some idea what they're doing when it comes to investing in property. It may be possible to fake a handful of awards, but a long, varied list of credentials generally correlates with true capabilities.

With over a decade of experience and accolades, a credible person will have the self-respect to admit when they are wrong. They will know how to show humility and back off when they encounter an area in which they cannot give accurate advice. They will recognize they aren't perfect and work on developing their credentials and learning from their mistakes. There aren't many unicorns out there with flawless track records, so if a person sounds too good to be true, they probably are not as credible as they claim to be.

How do you Assess Someone's Credibility?

It can be challenging to gauge whether a person's credentials are legitimate. As with intentions, the best way to judge good credibility is by looking at someone's reputation. To be one of your advisors a person should have earned a good reputation with a series of diverse accolades and awards over a long period of time. They should possess at least a ten year track record.

A reputation of good credibility is like a credit score. It takes years of paying bills on time to get a good credit score, but only a few missed payments to tank it. A person can lose their credibility quickly if they do something shady. Take Mina Chang and Power Balance for example. After they publicly admitted their discreditable actions, their careers were over. Mina certainly won't get another high level position with the government because now every-one knows she's a snake in the grass. Power Balance bracelets vanished from shelves around the world and hardly anyone noticed.

It's easy for people to fool you in the short term, but not in the long term. People with bad credentials get caught eventually. For this reason, assessing credentials means reviewing converging evidence from multiple sources over a long period of time to see the facts back up a person's claims.

One way to do this is with a background check. Look into the places someone claims to have associates and verify that they actually did what they claimed to do. Ask their friends to validate their credentials. Further, ask for a demonstration of their skills and be sure to have a third party evaluator in the room to confirm this individual is not blowing smoke. Make sure they don't have blindspots and they'll make sure you don't have blindspots.

And don't forget about motives. Even advisors with seemingly perfect cre-dentials might not be a good fit if they use their credentials unethically. Take the example of academic fraud.

Physician Andrew Wakefield came from a background of successful doc-tors. His father was a neurologist and his mother was a general practitioner. He studied medicine and earned his certification in 1981 and garnered pro-fessional accolades in 1993 when he published reports of the measles virus causing Crohn's disease, which was later disproved. Nonetheless, he earned a fellowship with the Royal College of Surgeons in 1985. In a 1998 study, Wakefield claimed that his research indicated a connection between autism and the measles-mumps-rubella vaccine. Coming from a reputable doctor with peer reviewed data, the research became respected and led many parents to refuse to vaccinate their children.

Ultimately, this led to increases in cases of measles and mumps, with some areas reporting widespread outbreaks. In a 2010 investigation, the public learned that Wakefield and his colleagues had altered facts about the children in their study. Wakefield had even been paid off by a lawyer planning to sue the manufacturer of the vaccine. However, the hysteria around vaccines has led parents to continue refusing to vaccinate their children ten years after his reports were proven to be falsified.

It doesn't matter if a person has some of the best-looking credentials in the world. If you don't properly assess the person behind the credentials, you might start listening to an advisor who is leading you astray. This demonstrates why intentions are just as important as credentials. You shouldn't let someone into your corner just because they have a solid resume or track record alone. You want both.

Everyone has a selfish bone in their body. Acknowledge this first. Don't feel guilty looking out for yourself, it's a natural human condition. When considering someone for your corner, the question is whether they can see a vision beyond the present moment. Do they act impulsively or do they keep working for a greater purpose?

If you wave a hamburger in front of your neighbors dog, he's going to eat it. But a police K-9 dog wouldn't because he has loyalty and training. He wants the burger too, but he can control the impulse. Are the people in your corner like the neighborhood dog or K-9? Do they act for themselves, or do they prioritize the long term value of healthy relationships?

Assembling Your Panel

You might think having a massive panel of experts will help you cover the most blindspots, but you really only need around five advisors at most. Five people is a good amount for a panel because you don't want too many cooks in the kitchen swaying you every which way. Among a hundred voices, you might start to listen to the most common advice instead of the most practical. Too much feedback can be a bad thing and lead you to second guessing yourself or overthinking things.

Google Ventures partner Jake Knapp finds that interviewing just five people exposes 85% of the problems with a new product. His method demonstrates that you don't need to talk to 1000 customers for qualitative feedback. He recommends having less than 7 people on your team of decision makers, otherwise you might suffer from too much input.

Human beings aren't meant to share their lives with hundreds of people. In hunter-gatherer days human tribes rarely exceeded 150 members. In our modern world, researchers find that we haven't changed much. While our digitally interconnected lives allow for us to connect with many individuals at once, we're truly only close with about 100 of them.

Of your 150 or fewer close allies, colleagues, and countrymen, you'd be lucky if 3% of them are fit to be in your corner. Finding these advisors is like searching for four-leaf clovers. When you evaluate people based on their credentials and motives, you'll find very few people in your life meet all the ideal criteria. Even if someone makes a promising candidate, you must put their blindspot detecting to the test before you let them into your corner.

You also want to assemble a team with a diverse range of credentials. When you have a variety of people with good motives and different credentials on your panel, you can cover the most blindspots at once and have foresight over a greater spectrum of challenges.

Remember, a person with strong credentials but weak motives is not an ideal candidate. You don't want someone like that in your corner. However, a person with slightly fewer credentials but a strong vision beyond the moment can still be an asset to you and team. You might not trust them with highly sensitive information, but you can position them in a way that lets their best abilities shine. They can gain credibility and experience over time, and still assist you in low stakes situations along the way.

How you position your team can make or break your cabinet. The example of the Battle of Cannae illustrates this. In this decisive battle, the Carthaginians and their allies, led by Hannibal, surrounded and practically annihilated a larger Roman and Italian army. It is regarded as one of the greatest tactical feats in military history and one of the worst defeats the Romans endured.

The Carthaginian army was a combination of warriors from numerous regions. It numbered about 40,000 to 50,000 Libyans, Gaetulians, Gauls, Iberians, Celtiberians, Lusitanians, Numidians, and Phoenicians. The army's uniting factor was the personal tie each group had with Hannibal. Hannibal was a great leader with intentions that aligned with those of his allies. Plus, he had a long and credible history of military savvy. Hannibal positioned his allies strategicly so that each of them could shine. They all had unique weapons, armor, and skills that had to be approached differently. On the other hand, the

Roman army was comprised mostly of a single type of fighter, heavy infantry, with identical standard equipment and formations. When you only have one type of fighter, you have a massive blindspot due to shared weaknesses.

Knowing the superiority of the Roman infantry, Hannibal instructed his light infantry to withdraw deliberately, creating a tight gap for the Roman heavy infantry to fill. Then, Hannibal's heavy infantry and ranged units could surround the Romans with a tight semicircle. By doing so, he turned the strength of the Roman infantry into a weakness. While the front ranks were gradually advancing, the bulk of the Roman troops began to lose their cohesion, as troops from the reserve lines advanced into the growing gaps. Soon they were compacted together so closely that they had little space to wield their weapons. The arms of Hannibal's flanking lines crushed the Romans and utterly defeated them.

The problem was that the Romans didn't cover their blindspots. They had a massive weakness in their poor mobility, yet they charged ahead because they thought their sheer numbers would be enough to win. A gorilla-sized blindspot sounds bad, but imagine having a blindspot the size of an army! If Rome had greater foresight through diversified strengths and credentials, they might not have fallen to Hannibal of Carthage.

We can point out weaknesses in clashing armies to visualize blindspots, but massive blindspots can occur in any group of collaborators no matter how mundane. If you're running a tech startup with a bunch of smart coders who excel at programming, but you don't have any marketing or sales experts to help you sell your product, all is lost. You can't have a football team made of all quarterbacks. If you don't diversify your advisors, you might have a shared blindspot that can set you back.

One way to decide which combination of experts can cover your blindspots is to identify where you need the most help. Next ask how your advisors' skills relate to those critical areas. Once all the big blindspots are accounted for, you can think about how to cover the more subtle ones. If there is an area of your life where you feel overconfident, get an advisor in your corner who can level you out and make sure you don't set your expectations too high. Sometimes the areas we think we're the best at managing are the places where we have the most blindspots.

If the opportunity arises, you want someone to help advise you on even the more insignificant areas of your life in case there's an underlying issue you've been overlooking. The objective of foresight is to decrease blindspots at all times, simultaneously building trust and respect in a way that protects your relationship with your cabinet members. Remember, you are also in their corner. So help them spot their own blindspots as well.

Competency is Just as Valuable as Connection

We look for different qualities in roommates than we do in our close friends. A good roommate knows how to stay on top of their finances, cleanliness, and other responsibilities, whereas a good friend might have Great Guy syndrome. Meaning, he's a "great guy" to hang out with on the weekends and joke around with, but would be a nightmare to live with for one reason or another.

Your close friends might be more interested in protecting your feelings than giving you critical feedback, so they might not be the most trustworthy blindspot detectors. Plus, if you have a lot in common, you likely have some shared weaknesses that neither of you can compensate for.

Teaming up with people who have different strengths, even if they aren't your friends, helps you increase your coverage of blindspots. That's why Lincoln assembled his cabinet the way he did. He valued people with the best expertise and range of knowledge over those who were his close friends.

How do you recruit people who you don't like to be on your panel? Be respectful of them and give them time and attention. Tell them there's something you admire about them and ask for their honest opinion. In turn, give them a piece of advice that you know will help them and do it respectfully so it doesn't come off as passive aggressive. Connect with the true value of what each of you brings to the relationship. If your positions as advisors prove to be mutually beneficial and your intentions are in the right places, you might end up like Lincoln, with rivals that turned into friends.

Signs of Growth

The final quality you need to look for when building your team is signs of growth. Observe which of your candidates work to fill blindspots when they arise, taking small steps instead of large leaps. These qualities indicate the potential for a thoughtful advisor who knows how to grow with you instead of against you. Gradually let these people into your circle and see how they adapt to fill your blindspots. You're likely not going to find top quality advisors right away, but if you can assess people's good intentions and credibility, you can help them develop into better teammates. Once they're on your team, help them build on their Imagination, Values, and Efficiency (three areas of life I'll introduce you to in the following chapters).

Being in Someone Else's Corner

Having people in your corner isn't a one way street. You're going to be in other people's corners as well. To be the best advisor for someone else, you must learn how to stay on the Track of Humility and operate with foresight. You must also have the same two fundamental qualities we've been discussing already: healthy motives and enriched credentials.

Harnessing healthy motives means wanting others to succeed. It means that you will speak up when you detect a problem and identify blindspots that others can't see. Your aim is to work with others and let them know feedback is meant to help them, not hurt them. You shouldn't be critical for any reason, but you may respectfully challenge your teammates to walk on the edge of discomfort as you provide the moral support they need in order to grow. Stay on this track no matter how much pushback or frustration you experience, as long as you know you are doing the three Rs—the Right things in the Right ways for the Right reasons. Sometimes when you receive pushback from the person you're trying to help, it is evidence they are struggling to stay on the Track of Humility. They might be in denial that they are falling off the Track. It is your responsibility to continue to push this person to stay on the Track.

Sometimes, when you are in someone's corner and they come to you for advice, you may not know how to help them. It is easy to give into the urge to offer advice for something that is beyond your expertise, justifying your support on the basis of trying to be a good friend. This, however, is to fail Abraham Lincoln's proverbial test of character.

When someone asks you for advice, they are momentarily putting you in a position of power. If you are unqualified to give the advice, then any advice you give is, at its core, self-serving. You are bolstering your own image in this person's eyes, rather than using your position to set them up for long term success. It would be better to admit you don't know how to help, rather than trying to sound intelligent. Your honesty is much more valuable to the longevity of the relationship than any advice you could give. That being said, your friend still needs help, so how can you ensure they get the best support possible?

In general, to ensure you have good credentials to advise others you must work at something persistently until you discover a working formula for success, and then test that formula repeatedly. Assemble legitimate data based on your methodology. Acquire the right paperwork to validate your success from credible communities. Some examples are accolades from peers, university degrees, and widely-accepted published findings. This might sound like an unreasonably high standard for helping a peer, but the truth is that this is the bare minimum required in order to obtain long term success. This is why many people go back to school in the middle of their careers; because they realize the long term value of true expertise.

You would become discreditable if you gave advice in areas that are not your expertise. You should be able to admit when you don't know how to help somebody instead of coming up with untested theories. It's ok to say "I don't know." Remember, the relationship is something you must protect it at all costs. Use your lack of knowledge to help your peer learn, as you too can learn new material. This will simultaneously reinforce your humility and expand your horizons.

Ultimately, if you stay on the Track of Humility, your motives and credentials should be in order and you can be a good advisor to others. However, you can still fall into traps, give poor advice, and fall off balance. Because of this it's important you continue to grow and improve.

Once you're part of a solid team and have good people to cover your blindspots, you should all grow together to develop your Imagination, build on your Values, and discover more Efficiencies to protect yourselves from falling into the traps on both sides of the Track of Humility.

To cultivate Imagination, you must become an artful challenger. Constantly challenge yourself and others to create scenarios that stimulate your inner spirit and theirs.

To practice Values, you must become disciplined and focused on what is most important at all times. Listen to your inner voice and the voices of others with empathy to align your behaviors with your beliefs before you take the next steps.

To improve Efficiency, you must become more aware of your decision making and learn to be an artful strategist. Realize that you must adopt a new lifestyle of learning to better understand your hopes and fears on this path. Learning must quench your thirst for growth. Experiment with different ways to execute your mutually agreed upon plan.

When you assemble the right team and are a good advisor for others, you operate with the Bright, Positive, Humble Attitude. You'll gain enhanced foresight and the ability to see the pitfalls ahead while your "presidential" cabinet checks for blindspots. You are setting up a healthy position for yourself and your team. Now to maintain it and stay on the Track of Humility, you will need to develop your Imagination, Values, and Efficiency on an ongoing basis. This is a lifelong practice.

But first, let's open your Emotions…

Chapter 5
Your Emotions

Emotional Tracks

Imagine you need to finish a big report before the end of the week and if you don't deliver on time, it could strain the relationship with your top client. You've been racing all day and haven't taken a break to serve your needs, so you head to the nearby diner work from a booth while you refuel. As you open the menu you get a call from the client. Answering, you nod to the waiter and point at the first thing you notice on the menu: mushrooms. The client needs your credit card number for a business expense. A moment later the waiter returns with a steaming bowl and you breathe a sigh of relief. He serves you a suspicious mushroom stew with a fish head sticking out of one end and a tail from the other. Before you can say anything, the client calls back to inform you the card isn't working. You check your wallet and realize you brought the wrong expense card to the diner. *What's going on today?* You pack up your stew and race back to the office, doomed to stomach the fishy bed you laid for yourself.

No one likes to make decisions under pressure. When we're stressed out or in an emotional state, we can experience lapses in judgement. Runaway emotions create blindspots, and without a rational and neutral perspective it's hard to make appropriate evaluations. This isn't to say that emotions are bad. It's human nature to feel a wide spectrum of emotions on a regular basis and we shouldn't try to suppress or overpower what we feel. Hopefully we're not operating as unfeeling robots, making every decision with a cold calculation. *Honey, I'm not sure if I love you, too. Let me run a regression analysis.*

We all know from personal experience that being emotionally-charged can lead to both shortsighted thinking and to our greatest discoveries. This chapter is about how to enhance your foresight by harnessing your emotions to work for you rather than against you.

Crimes of Passion

In 2010, three Belgian skydivers found themselves in a high-stakes love triangle. A married mother of two was in an affair with her skydiving instructor, Marcel. He was caught by *another* one of his skydiving romances, a woman in her twenties. The next day, Marcel took his two lovers out for a skydive. The mother's parachute never opened and she fell two miles, dying on impact. The younger woman was charged with cutting her lines before the jump. Jealous of her competition, the twenty-something skydiver snuffed the other woman out with deadly sabotage.

The judge in this case gave the killer thirty years in prison instead of life, citing her fragile psychological state for the reduced sentence. Crimes of passion typically receive shorter sentences than other homicides as intense emotional circumstances are considered a partial excuse for murder. I'm not here to debate whether this is fair, but I do want to note that many of these crimes would not have happened if the perpetrators had stayed in the neutral zone. Feelings of anger, jealousy, betrayal, and fear can be overwhelming, and may require excruciating effort to process. Rash decisions made when we are on one of these emotional tracks can lead to horrible, deadly outcomes. If Marcel's jealous lover had processed her pain more effectively she probably wouldn't be in prison, and a death could have been avoided.

Insecurity

There's an unsettling Wikipedia page that documents over 200 hazing-related deaths in American fraternities. These deaths were all accidents, but their prevalence points to a bigger underlying issue. The most common cause of fraternity hazing deaths since the year 2000 is alcohol poisoning, often related to peer pressure. To fit in with the social club, new members feel they must drink a potentially lethal amount of alcohol or face being rejected. They're operating from a place of insecurity. They want to be liked by their peers, so they do what they're told and don't resist when they're uncomfortable. They want everyone to cheer when they complete a drinking challenge so they can earn respect. They don't want to look like losers.

The pressure to fit in takes people off the Track of Humility. It creates a blindspot that prevents critical self-evaluation. When alcohol is added to the mix, people can die. They stop listening to the warning signs in their bodies and prioritize the desire to belong over their own wellbeing. An emotional track of insecurity can lead to flawed and potentially deadly decisions.

Overconfidence

On November 3rd, 1948, the *Chicago Tribune* incorrectly declared New York Governor Thomas Dewey the next U.S. President with the preemptive front-page headline "Dewey Defeats Truman." This slip-up wasn't a fringe opinion from an overzealous media outlet. Many U.S. newspapers had predicted Dewey's victory since early on in the presidential race and were standing by to print similar headlines on election day. However, underdog Harry Truman became the 33rd president because he didn't rest on his laurels during the campaign.

Dewey was overconfident and ran a safe, uninspiring campaign reported by the press that already supported him. He took things easy because his Republican party was strong while the Democraic party was splintered. He wasn't breaking his back to win the election. He thought it was already in the bag. Meanwhile, Truman felt like his back was against the wall.

Truman had to play it smart to beat his opponent and devise the most impactful way to reach voters. Rather than campaign with the media that didn't support him, Truman hit the road. His 22,000-mile "whistle stop" campaign put him right in front of American audiences all over the country so he could engage without media spin. These cross-country rallies were wildly successful in gaining support and firing up crowds. *Give him Hell, Harry!* was the popular battlecry. Dewey lost a favorable election because he was on a laid back, overconfident emotional track that led him into the Grandiose Mindset and a distorted view of reality.

The Neutral Emotional Track

The Track of Humility is the neutral emotional track. That's where we want to be to make appropriate evaluations and better decisions. But none of us are in the neutral zone 100% of the time. Actually, we're constantly swerving away from it.

On a daily basis, thousands of internal and external factors influence our mood. We're thankful we get to sleep in, but we feel guilty about not starting our day earlier. We're bored during the commute to work, but we're delighted when we arrive and a colleague smiles and says good morning. These shifts in mood are natural and won't necessarily pull us off the neutral emotional track, but if we get wrapped up in any of them we can start to veer off course without realizing it.

It's like driving down the highway. You can't stay in the center of your lane without making constant adjustments. When you feel the car start to drift in one direction or another, you can bring yourself back to center. However, when you're heavily influenced by strong emotions, you can swerve off the Track of Humility onto another emotional track (and maybe end up snipping someone's parachute release cords). We want to avoid being pulled onto emotional tracks because they are riddled with pitfalls.

Emotional Pitfalls

Every emotional track is comprised of two competing forces: Hope for Gain and Fear of Loss.

Negative emotions like sadness, disgust, and boredom can pull us down the Fear of Loss emotional track, which revolves around worry and anxiety. The Hope for Gain emotional track is linked to emotions like joy, surprise, and confidence. When you go down one of these emotional tracks, you create blindspots that can lead you into the pitfalls. Here's how:

Grandiosity Mindset

Hope for Gain: Thomas Dewey was so excited about winning the election that he overlooked the success of his rival's campaign and lost. His overconfidence pulled him off the Track of Humility and he fell into the pitfall of grandiose thinking.

Fear of Loss: Incoming fraternity members are afraid of social rejection so they become emotional and veer off the neutral track onto the Fear of Loss track. Their grandiose thinking leads them to engage in drinking events they think they can handle, but their expectations don't line up with the reality of alcohol poisoning.

Entitlement Mindset

Hope for Gain: Buddy Holly was excited to finish the Winter Dance Party tour no matter what. This led him off the Track of Humility and onto the entitlement trap, which caused him to avoid taking responsibility for the problems with the tour.

Fear of Loss: After a series of fruitless dates, some people become afraid they aren't attractive. To protect their self-concept, they might shift the blame for the bad dates to others. *It must be that no one I've dated has been good enough for me. It's not my fault it's not working out.* Affirming their own grandiosity out of fear makes them blind to the entitlement trap. This causes them to shift blame and prevents them from being able to learn from their failures.

Charlatan Mindset

Hope for Gain: When the General Artists Corporation managed the Winter Dance Party tour, the executives were excited to make a big profit and disregarded the health and safety concerns raised by the touring bands. They accepted no blame for the horrible scheduling and ultimate plane crash. Instead, they asked the remaining musicians to keep touring. Their excitement pulled them off the Track of Humility and got them so focused on profitability they were blind to their charlatanism.

Fear of Loss: Mina Chang forged fake credentials to apply for high-profile jobs and feared that she wasn't good enough to get hired on her own. Instead of earning her credentials legitimately, she decided to pretend she was a qualified leader out of fear. As her illusion grew bigger, she couldn't see that she was falling right into the charlatan trap.

Despair Mindset

Hope for Gain: Marla is excited to quit cigarettes, but falls into deep despair every time she puts down the pack. She doesn't truly want to quit. When she isn't smoking she feels like she's missing out and torturing herself. Because the idea of being smoke-free is so exciting she keeps getting pulled off the Track of Humility and caught in the despair trap.

Fear of Loss: Bronze medalists are happier than silver medalists because they're excited about getting on the podium whereas many silver medalists are fixated on falling short of the gold. Their fear of losing pulls them onto a negative emotional track and blinds them to the fact that they are falling into the despair trap.

Excuses Mindset

Hope for Gain: When an overconfident singer gets ridiculed by judges' nasty reviews during a talent show, he might be so excited about his perceived singing talent that he'll deflect the negative criticism. Instead of thinking, *I should reevaluate my singing ability,* he thinks, *I'm a perfectly good singer. These judges have no idea what they're talking about.* This is just one example of how positive emotions can pull us off the Track of Humility and into the excuses trap.

Fear of Loss: When you see the Joneses come home in a shiny new car and realize that Mr. Jones got the job you were after, you might feel afraid that you're not good enough to make the same accomplishments. On this negative emotional track, you might come up with excuses. *I'm just as good, he must have been lucky. I never wanted that job anyway.* Fearful emotional tracks can blind you to the fact that you are falling into the excuses pitfall.

Discreditable Mindset

Hope for Gain: Positive emotions can also tempt us to lie to ourselves and others when they pull us off the Track of Humility and into the discreditable trap. Tabloid publishers might sell more copies when they use exaggerated content. If they're too invested in the positive emotions of feeling like a success, they'll continue to make up stories until their readers find out they're discreditable and stop buying.

Also, many times when you meet someone and they don't want to discuss their gray past, it's because they want to continue living a double life for as long as they can. By suppressing the dirty details they hope to slide on through and keep doing what they know they shouldn't be doing. It's only a matter of time before their house of cards will come tumbling down, but they can't see it because they've been carried off on a high emotional track and they are blind to the trap.

Fear of Loss: When a person is afraid of disagreeing with their peers, they might flip-flop their opinion depending on who they're talking to, hoping not to offend anyone. When others catch on they will lose trust and respect for this person. For someone who is caught in the discreditable trap, the fear of letting others down can unconsciously provoke them to lie as a means of defense.

Emotional tracks can shape our decisions by creating blindspots that hide the traps. As we are pulled further away from the Track of Humility we can grow even more emotional. As a result, spending too much time on an emotional track can have lasting effects on our behavior.

Emotional Tracks Shape Your Life

Both positive and negative emotions can distort our perception of reality and lead to ineffective choices. The more time we spend on an emotional track, the more its distortions start to feel normal. Consistently operating on an emotional track forms habits that become hard to break. After many years of this it will require immense effort to return to the Track of Humility.

One reason it's so easy to get locked onto an emotional track is a phenomenon called state-dependent memory. This refers to one of the ways our brain organizes information. Various studies have demonstrated that if we learn a piece of information in a certain psychological state, we are more likely to recall that information when we are in the same state again. Researchers have supported this concept by getting lab rats loaded on a host of medical-grade drugs.

In the 90s, some scientists named Jackson, Koek, and Colpaert put rats into a series of mazes that tested their memory. Some rats were high on drugs such as ketamine or ecstasy when they learned the shape of the maze while others were sober. When retested, the strung out rodents were better at solving the maze if they were injected with the same drugs again. These rats help explain why you can only find that one late-night pizza place when you're drunk at three in the morning. It's easier to recall things when you're in the same emotional state you were in when you learned them.

This phenomenon has been demonstrated in studies involving language as well. Bilingual people are able to recall more information when tested in the same language they used to learn the material. Another set of researchers, Godden and Baddeley, demonstrated that context matters too. In 1975, they tested the role of context in memory with scuba divers. In this experiment, they asked the divers to learn a list of words either on land or underwater. Then, they quizzed the divers' memory of the list in either the same or the opposite situation. The result was similar to other state-dependent memory studies. The divers' memory was better when they were tested in the same context in which they had originally learned the words. If you're having trouble remembering what to pick up from the grocery store, try to picture where you created your grocery list (and what language you used) to help jog your memory. If you were high when you made the list it might help to shop in the same state too.

This phenomenon of state-dependent memory also explains how emotional tracks can hold us captive. People who learn information when they are in a certain mood find it easier to recall these memories when they are tested in the same mood. Further, it is easier to recall unpleasant memories when we're sad and pleasant memories when we're happy. For this reason, a fearful emotional track will make fearful memories more present, frequent, and relevant to our brains, even when they aren't helpful.

If we're paranoid that something bad will happen on our walk home, we will start to remember situations in which we were paranoid before. We'll recall all the stories we've ever heard about walkers being attacked. The sound of a door closing won't seem like someone innocently returning home for the night, but a masked murderer stepping outside to get us. When you see a dog, you won't remember playing with puppies in a daisy field, you'll think about the one time you got bitten.

When we live on a certain emotional track, memories formed when we were in that emotional state flood our consciousness. This can lead us to jump to irrational conclusions. Our appraisals become flawed while the memories grow stronger as we feel increasingly emotional. On a positive emotional track, thoughts of success are bountiful while worries of failure are harder to find. Under these circumstances, we might overestimate an outcome, blind to the possibility of undesirable alternatives. When we get in the habit of thinking *"What's the worst that could happen?"* instead of evaluating actual risks, we remain on an emotional track riddled with hidden pitfalls.

Long term potentiation (LTP) adds fuel to the fire. LTP is the strengthening of neural connections as result of frequent stimulation. The more we remember certain feelings or ideas, the more vivid, efficient, and habitual these memories become. After years of depression, our brains might build an information superhighway to those pessimistic thoughts we've been ruminating on, while paths to positive memories become unmaintained and difficult to traverse. LTP is why emotional tracks grow more powerful and captivating the longer we dwell on them.

Further, heightened emotional states such as excitement and fear make our memories more potent and more susceptible to LTP. One of the most important neurotransmitters involved in memory is glutamate, which is secreted during moments of stress. Stressful situations make our memories stronger due to a flood of glutamate. Therefore, the positive and negative emotional tracks can be more influential on our memories, thoughts, and experiences than the neutral track. This is partially why both positive and negative forms of anxiety are unproductive. An exciting or terrifying situation can be many times more memorable than a neutral experience, making it easy to drift onto an emotional track and stay there.

Our brains are wired to remember information we learned on the emotional tracks better than information we learn on the neutral track. The salience of emotional memories can lead to long term potentiation, which creates irrational evaluations. We begin to place more value on the thoughts that are relevant to our current emotional state instead of considering all of the facts equally.

The more time we spend caught up in these emotional cognitions, the more they shape our lives. We might end up locked on an emotional track bound for countless pitfalls, which we're blind to because we want to protect our ego. In feeding our ego instead of making more rational evaluations, we reinforce unhealthy behavior. Our senses distort the world to reflect how we feel instead of taking in everything as it really is. These powerful psychological forces make getting out of the pitfalls and back onto the neutral track tremendously challenging.

Importantly, emotions aren't the bad guy here. Feeling excited or afraid won't necessarily set us up to get caught in the traps. If we respond to our emotions in a healthy way by letting them run their course before making a decision, we can make sure to always act from the neutral track.

So how do we deal with intense emotions without suppressing them? It's called mastering the neutral state and it's one of my greatest tools for staying on the Track of Humility. Now that we understand the role of the other emotional tracks, we can discuss how to subvert their pull and stay neutral.

The Neutral State

The two emotional tracks that pull us away from center, Hope for Gain and Fear of Loss, are opposite sides of the same coin. Staying neutral is about learning to balance on the fine line of energy between the two poles. Imagine holding two magnets a quarter of an inch apart. There is palpable energy between them, but it is invisible to the naked eye. The Track of Humility is the space where you can use that energy to propel you forward with superior decision making.

The Hope for Gain and Fear of Loss tracks can heighten emotions in either a positive or negative direction. The neutral state is the area found between these extremes. To stay in the middle of these poles and propel ourselves towards our goals in a healthy way, we can utilize presence, patience, perceptions, the twenty percent rule, and the people in our corner.

Presence

Hope for gain and fear of loss only exist in the future, so one secret to help you remain neutral is to focus on the present. For example, if you are up for a promotion, you might be hopeful about the increased responsibility and pay. However, you could fear a reduction in your quality of life as you fill bigger shoes and have to sacrifice more of your time for the job. Both excitement and fear can lead to poor decisions that impact your ability to secure the promotion at all. If you're too hopeful you might go gallivanting around the office like you own the place and your overconfidence could indicate you're not ready for such a big position. On the other hand, if you're too fearful you might slack off in your current position because you're preoccupied with fears of the big workload in your future. Straying off the Track of Humility as a result of focusing on the future can lead you to make irrational decisions in the present that screw up your trajectory, which is what happened to Thomas Dewey in 1948.

Fear of loss and hope of gain are emotions about a future that may or may not come to pass. Focusing on the present rather than the future will reduce these feelings and help you stay on the neutral track. Instead of reacting to the thought of something that hasn't happened, stick to evaluating real and present information. This way you can stay between the positive and negative emotional poles, accurately weigh the pros and cons when sizing up a situation, and take the proper steps to line up your goals with reality.

Patience

Patience is another virtue that will keep you in the neutral state, which is why we should never go shopping on an empty stomach. When we're hungry, we often respond to our cravings and buy too much food rather than picking up only the groceries we need. Hunger takes us off the neutral track and influences us to shop irrationally. However, if we are patient, we can slow down to feed ourselves before going to the store. This way we will be able to scan the shelves from a neutral emotional state, make different decisions, and purchase an appropriate quantity of food instead of loading up on enough chips and salsa to feed a small village.

The application of this logic goes beyond grocery shopping. If you're stressed out at work, you might not be in a neutral state of mind. This makes it challenging to have a conversation with an underperforming employee without getting angry at him. To get back to neutral, you might take a soothing walk away from the office or postpone your meeting until the next day so you can manage your stress in a healthy way.

If you're fired up about going on a date but don't have the patience to calm yourself down before arranging the plans, you might make a critical error like telling your date to meet you at a restaurant outside of its operating hours. Taking the time to manage your emotions can help you navigate exciting and frightening situations while remaining neutral.

But what if you have to make a big decision on the spot and there is no time to process how you feel? You might encounter a time-sensitive ultimatum: either take the last ticket to the game now or let someone else have it. It's a tough choice, especially since you already have dinner plans with your girlfriend, but you need to decide now. When you can't process the situation with patience and your emotions start weighing on what you should do, I suggest identifying the greatest risk and considering how you might handle its loss.

In this example, if you skip the game you'll miss a fun night out with your friends. You also won't be able to see your team perform live until next season, and your friends might feel let down that you won't be there. On the other hand, skipping dinner with your girlfriend might lead to a disappointed partner, conflict at home, and a few nights of sleeping on the couch. What's the greatest loss and how might you handle it?

The answer to this question will vary, but the strategy of identifying and avoiding the worst loss will help you make a more neutral decision when you're short on time. Also, it's important to note that your evaluation of the loss will be skewed by your emotions, which is why it's good to have people in your corner who can help you make an appraisal in a pinch. Proper evaluation also explains why perception is a huge factor in remaining neutral.

Perception

When we're excited, we overvalue positive outcomes and underplay negative outcomes. Contrarily, when we're feeling down, we overemphasize downsides and disregard upsides.

This makes it difficult to discern between actual losses and perceived losses. Maybe your girlfriend will be relieved to cancel dinner and the risks to your relationship were completely in your head. To better calculate losses when you're in a highly emotional state, you must rely on factual information. Try to verify your assumptions by asking the people in your corner what they think. Stick to facts you gathered while you were in a neutral state. Recognize that anything you learn or assume while emotional is going to be a skewed version of the truth.

Another technique to prevent emotional tracks from skewing your perceptions is to ask yourself *"What if I'm wrong?"* in every situation. If you're operating with fear, ask yourself what would happen if there's really nothing to worry about and everything is going to work out fine. This can help you stay more realistic in your appraisals. Conversely, if you're certain something great will happen, remind yourself that you could be wrong and everything could go horribly awry. This mental exercise might not resolve your heightened emotions, but it will help you return to a more neutral evaluation of a situation before you make a choice.

Twenty Percent Emotional Investment

Emotional investment makes it hard to stay neutral. When we go over the Twenty Percent Rule we become averse to loss and might ignore the possibility of an undesirable outcome.

To stay under the 20% line, we shouldn't suppress our emotions, but entertain them. Fighting emotions only makes us more invested. We must instead allow an emotion to run its course and fade away. It might turn out to only last for a few minutes. However, trying to fight an emotion makes it grow stronger and last longer. Bottling something in can heighten stress, and before you know it your emotional investment can climb to well over 20%.

If you can allow your emotions to arise and move on in a healthy way through meditation, counseling, and other activities that bring you back to neutral, you won't become emotionally overinvested and lock yourself into an irrational emotional track.

People in Your Corner

When you think you're on the Track of Humility, it's wise to double check with the people in your corner to see if you have missed any blind spots. We all have a variety of emotional blindspots that lead us to act before thinking. Subtle unconscious shifts in our emotions can influence our biases and behaviors without us noticing. When the people in our corner keep us in check, we can make the correct adjustments to stay neutral and better train our ability to stay on the Track of Humility. Like Lincoln, we can use experts in other fields to ensure we're processing information in a rational way that allows for better decisions.

However, we can't go to the people in our corner for every decision we make. If we're in line at the drive-through and we're afraid of making the wrong choice off the value menu, we shouldn't have to phone a friend. Our close advisors don't have the time or availability to check in with us so frequently. Instead, I suggest working out a cadence to regularly meet with your cabinet. Perhaps you could schedule two or three meetings week to check in and go over different aspects of your lives. During highly emotional times, take a page out of Lincoln's book and create an open door approach with your trusted few. Emotions can be heightened by a new opportunity, a breakup, a deadline, or a celebration, and when these situations threaten to pull you off the Track of Humility, daily meetings could be appropriate.

The bottom line is that you should be able to rely on the people in your corner and they should be able to rely on you as a lifeline, personal consultant, and sponsor. Be there for each other when you and your cabinet need one another. These relationships are symbiotic, but you should always work toward being more self-sufficient as well. Learn to master the neutral state using the tools of presence, patience, perception, and the Twenty Percent Rule before you call your advisor from the drive-through line.

Using these techniques, you can master the neutral state to combat both positive and negative emotions and stay on the Track of Humility.

Chapter 6
Imagination

So far this book has focused on what *not* to do so you can navigate around pitfalls and stay on the Track of Humility.

We've seen it's problematic to overestimate yourself because you'll risk falling into the Grandiose Mindset. Despite what your parents may have told you about shooting for the stars, I am telling you to shoot for what is in reach to make real progress.

We've also seen that if you invest more than 20% of yourself in anything you'll risk losing yourself to uncertainties. Despite what your middle school gym coach might have told you about giving it all you've got and never giving up, I am telling you to set a boundary on your commitments. Save enough emotional resources for all areas of your life, rather than going all-in on any one endeavor.

And we've seen the problems with acting while we're emotional. Despite what the self-help books might say about trusting your emotions and going with your gut, I'm telling you that emotions pull you off the Track of Humility. Instead of making an important decision in an emotional state, find a way to calm yourself down so you can act from a neutral state.

We've discussed many things we can *avoid* to stay on the Track of Humility, but there's more to achieving perfect foresight than steering out of harm's way. We must now discuss what we *should* do to stay on the right track. Instead of operating from a place of avoidance, it's critical to evaluate what elements we should embrace to achieve our desired outcomes. In my experience, there are three elements, or positive mindsets, that keep us out of the Dark, Negative Attitude and propel us towards our goals.

The Three Elements to master are Imagination, Values, and Efficiency. You want to cultivate them in yourself and in the people in your corner. In this chapter, we are going to be discussing the first Element, Imagination.

Imagination isn't about writing a new fantasy novel or inventing a new type of toothpaste, it's about creating a healthy mindset as it pertains to your vision. You can use the power of creative brainstorming to identify the stepping stones you must walk on your journey towards your long term goals. We must use our imagination to create a plan of action and tackle the next step on the way to our dreams.

Take caution, though, because Imagination has two faces: a productive side, and a destructive side. Imagination creates a world that does not exist, which can be helpful if it motivates us to make a plan for how to get from where we are to where we idealistically want to be. In fact, every goal you've ever set for yourself originated in your Imagination. A healthy Imagination leads us to envision new possible versions of our future selves. We might picture ourselves as a doctor, or a new parent, being more charming, twenty pounds lighter, and living in our dream vacation home.

Sometimes our wildest dreams are more attainable than we think, so we shouldn't rule out lofty goals as impossible. Achieving them is a great aspiration. But we must accept that we don't know how long it will take or what all the necessary steps will be to get there. By maintaining authentic self-esteem, self-confidence, and integrity, and letting those characteristics drive our behavior, we can build a path forward. Furthermore, a healthy environment can stimulate our Imagination, which helps us develop a wide range of potential pathways to our goals and devise solutions that might not be obvious.

As we brainstorm about how to achieve our goals, we can fuel our Imagination to creatively develop a myriad of options for our next steps.

Throughout the process, consider reflecting, *Are these ideas relevant? Am I distorting reality to align with my goal?* Find creative ideas for achieving your goals, never give up on meaningful people and projects, and keep the end in mind to use Imagination to your benefit.

Imagination becomes destructive when we operate on it alone. There are infinite future versions of ourselves, so we have to understand what is fueling our desire for one particular version. While we can set out to accomplish anything, assuming we know how to reach any goal can lead us into the Grandiose Mindset. You can't simply say, "I will become the boss of my company," without taking any steps to make your goal a reality.

When our Imagination produces big ideas without tangible plans of action, we can get wrapped up in illusions. These illusions can take us off course and derail us from pursuing a goal.

Falling short of an imagined goal because we don't know how to realize, it can shatter our confidence and self-worth. We often operate from an unconscious mental state and assume we understand the initial steps in our process better than we really do. This can cause us to get ahead of ourselves and start working on "Step 4" before "Step 1." In other words, we can put the cart before the horse.

Imagination can be destructive instead of productive when we fail to outline our path and sample our progress along the way.

To build a healthy Imagination mindset, I use the following six prompts:

1. Stimulate inner dialogue without judgment
2. Temper your arrogance and build on your confidence
3. Look beyond yourself and work on being selfless
4. Covert your passions into visions beyond self-interest
5. Challenge the people in your corner to grow alongside you
6. Redefine your feelings of fear by leveraging them to identify what is meaningful to you

I'll explain the meaning of these prompts and how they keep you on the Track of Humility. But first, there is a Step Zero. A prerequisite to ensure we're operating with a positive, authentic attitude—one that is humble and not amped up by hype—so we can choose the correct paths to attain our envisioned goals.

Step Zero – The Naked Test

What's your diet? Do you exercise? Are you doing the work you enjoy? If money weren't an issue, what would you be doing? Your gut reaction to these questions will be positive or negative based on how self-aware you are. A negative reaction might indicate that you're falling short in one or more areas of your life and you lack a plan of action to get yourself to a positive place. A positive reaction tends to reflect alignment, confidence, self-worth, and personal responsibility. Whether or not your life is "perfect," if you can honestly identify what's working in your life and what needs work, you're operating with a positive mindset that encourages healthy growth towards a better future self (you).

This is where the Naked Test works as an attitude barometer. By yourself, get naked in front of a mirror. What do you see? Are you happy with yourself? Ask, *What are the things I can change to become happier with the reflection? Are the things tapping away in the back of my mind like a woodpecker based on how others see me, or are they things I want to work through for me and only me?*

These inquiries are both physical and mental. Physically, we can assess how we look and whether we're happy with how we treat our bodies. Mentally, we need to check out level of positivity. To assess mental positivity we can ask ourselves questions like:

- Am I humble at my core, or just as a front?
- Am I faithful when no one is looking?
- Am I balanced at home and at work, giving respectful attention to both?
- Do I give attention to myself in order to be more for others?
- Do I speak with intelligence and take time to do necessary research and learning?

- Do I take time for others, especially when nothing is in it for me?

- Do I take advantage of others, or steal the credit from others' creations?

- Do I look at someone else's plate at a restaurant and think, *I should have ordered that!* Before I even try the meal placed in front of me?

- Do I drive through the neighborhood, envious of other houses on the block and assume that only thieves could afford such massive estates?

- Do I look at an exotic vehicle stopped at a light and mutter ill thoughts about a person I don't even know?

If we are experiencing any hallmarks of the Dark, Negative Attitude such as anger, jealousy, insecurity, or inattention, we are likely operating with a poor-me, self-entitled mindset that must be evaluated and adjusted right away. If the Naked Test reveals that you have a negative disposition, the best way to change it is to take responsibility for your current position. Realize that the choices you have made led you to this position and new choices can lead you out of it. We cannot simply will ourselves into a positive attitude, but we can take productive steps to become happy with who we see in the mirror. The difficulty is that the Dark, Negative Attitude can influence us to pick the wrong, shortcut paths to security, confidence, and a positive self-image. These shortcuts are often a massive waste of time and effort that leads us right back to where we started.

A healthy Imagination will help you brainstorm your way out of a corner, but positivity is crucial for deciding which path to take to achieve your desired outcome. So how can you pick a positive path when you're bogged down with negativity? Take a look at Step One...

1. Challenge Yourself to Stimulate Inner Dialogue

Stimulating your inner dialogue begins with quieting all your fears, hopes, and prejudices to leave you with a blank mental slate. This process is known as compartmentalization. Even if you are in a negative mindset, compartmental-ization will allow you to put your doubts aside so you can freely entertain any idea that comes up.

You can accomplish compartmentalization by acting as a problem solver instead of a worrier. Imagine you need to come up with $200 by the end of the week or else you'll default on a loan and your credit score will plummet. A worrier might start to rule out options. *Borrowing it is out because I can't be coming off as needy or dependent. And I can't steal the money because that's illegal.* They wouldn't entertain selling their old Pokémon card collection though, because those cards mean more to them than going bankrupt. By mentally shooting down the ideas as we have them, we limit our imagination and inhibit our ability to solve problems.

During a brainstorming phase we should have no shame cycling through any conceivable approach to achieve the goal. This means momentarily re-moving any personal attachments or preconceived notions about which ideas are good and which are bad. Not allowing ourselves to entertain all possible paths forward handcuffs our imagination and keeps us trapped in a mental loop.

Another way to challenge our inner dialogue and come up with more cre-ative solutions is to eliminate the concept of competition. When you operate from a competitive mindset your Imagination will be hampered by negativity and judgment. You'll think about how to put your rival down instead of how to improve your own progress. You'll value yourself in terms of how your boss appraises you instead of how you appraise yourself. Further, you'll be satisfied with merely beating your competition rather than aiming for maximizing your potential, regardless of the bottom line. Your Imagination will be restricted to aggressive or dependent pathways instead of options that lead you to your goal through self-growth.

Competition is a form of judgement that inhibits healthy Imagination. Plaques and awards are monuments of past performance that collect dust. The real trophy is in letting go of the past to free your Imagination.

To brainstorm properly you must put away preconceived notions and self-judgments. This can be accomplished by forgetting about past experiences.

Thinking about your prior successes and failures might lead you to improperly jump to conclusions about how good or bad the ideas are. By overvaluing one pathway, you might disregard other, potentially more effective options. If you assume you know what will happen, you will become less creative.

This effect can be exemplified by comparing the creativity of a five-year-old to a fifty-year-old. If you were to ask a five-year-old to describe a certain building they would come up with dozens of wild and fresh descriptions. Perhaps a king and queen live inside and there's a tiger cage in the basement. A grown adult would be far more narrow in their description. "It's a three-story apartment building that needs a fresh coat of paint." Our life experiences have gradually stifled our Imagination.

To counter this dream killing bias, avoid banking on what you experienced in the past and try to view every challenge as brand new. To train your creativity and stimulate your inner dialogue, compartmentalize your judgements and brainstorm with a clean slate.

These mental exercises might be difficult at first. It's natural to ascribe judgment to your thoughts as they arise. We tend to want to save time and effort by paying attention to what allowed us to succeed in the past, and we avoid considering thoughts that make us uncomfortable. This is not conducive to a healthy inner dialogue. Learn to give yourself permission to put all judgments aside and let your creativity loose.

To challenge your creativity, put each idea on the table without judging it as good or bad. This isn't the time for evaluations. This is the time to compartmentalize so you can express the full range of your Imagination. Don't stress over ideas that seem ineffective at first. We'll get to that when we discuss Values and Efficiencies in the next two chapters. For now, everything is possible.

2. Challenge your Confidence to Avoid Resting on Your Laurels

Once we've identified every possible option through healthy, nonjudgmental Imagination, we can consider which pathways will be most effective for achieving our goals. However, the analysis of our ideas can be thrown off by our confidence. Our instinct is to use methods that worked in the past to overcome current challenges. We tend to rest on our laurels because it's easier for us to be confident in past success than it is to challenge ourselves to try something new. Our confidence leads us to overvalue past decisions that led to desirable outcomes and undervalue decisions that led to undesirable outcomes. However, in doing this it is easy to confuse a successful outcome with a successful process. Confidence can also cause us to ignore other factors that could be influencing our present circumstances.

Resting on our laurels because something worked for us before is like putting blinders on: We only see the same, familiar path right in front of us, and we don't bother to look around for alternatives.

As this mode of thinking stifles creativity, it can also dampen decision making. Sometimes approaching a new challenge with the same techniques works out perfectly, but other times it doesn't. Instead of being confident that we can judge a likely outcome based on the past, we should approach every challenge as a totally unique situation. This way, we can develop solutions independent of previous challenges and avoid being locked into an overconfident mindset that takes us off the Track of Humility and into Grandiosity.

Early success can cause us to grow Grandiose, imagining we can tackle anything that comes our way because we've experienced similar challenges before. When it doesn't work out, it comes as a massive blow to our self-confidence. Often we don't even consider we might have taken the wrong approach. Instead, we tell ourselves we must not be good enough.

Failure is typical and healthy. When you accept that, you can keep your confidence in check in the face of loss. You can get up, go back to the drawing board, and draw up a new plan of action. Taking failure as a sign of weakness or ineptitude will make you insecure and indecisive. Accept that the future is unknowable. With foresight you'll get more comfortable navigating the unknown.

Impulsive decisions based on a false sense of self-confidence come from insecurities, whereas asking questions that challenge your confidence comes from a secure place. It takes courage to consider the possibility that you're completely off-track with your approach to overcoming a challenge. Healthy confidence means you're looking for the right questions before searching for the right answers.

Devising questions that test your confidence will strengthen your research, discipline, and commitment generating solutions. Just as resistance training makes your body stronger, resisting the inclination to go with a confident gut feeling by introducing critical questions will make you emotionally stronger.

3. Look Beyond Yourself to Generate Ideas that Drive Innovative Solutions

Once you have compartmentalized your judgments and tempered your initial confidence in your solutions, you can further train your Imagination by searching beyond yourself. You may be a brainiac with a dozen unique approaches to a problem, but there are always more potential solutions. By utilizing others' perspectives, you can imagine innovative new ways to pursue your goals that you never could have conceived of on your own.

Imagine a group of people need to cross a river to get to town, but the bridge is out. A civil engineer might approach this problem through the lens of physics and construction, causing them to look for ways to rebuild the bridge using nearby materials like a fallen tree. An athlete might test the current of the water and suggest simply swimming to the other side. A bird trainer might call for help via carrier pigeon. Would a civil engineer come up with a solution that involves tying a note to a bird's foot? It's unlikely, yet it might be the fastest way to get the resources necessary to overcome the challenge ahead.

Everyone has a different set of skills, experiences, and perspectives that influence and limit their problem solving. There are some excellent solutions to problems that simply don't occur to us, so it's crucial to survey different people to generate possibilities we're unaware of. This is where the people in your corner can be an invaluable resource. As Lincoln used his cabinet of rivals to cover his blindspots, you too should get a diverse panel of experts in your corner to help you see solutions that you'd otherwise miss.

Conversations aren't the only source of new perspectives to generate ideas. The Internet, literature, and artwork can spark inspiration too. Sometimes walking around an art gallery or hitting the "random article" button of Wikipedia can put you in front of your solution by happenstance. It's healthy to open your mind to all schools of thought because inspiration can arise from the most unexpected places.

Once I was driving towards a drawbridge over the mouth of a harbor during an ice storm. The water had frozen solid, trapping cargo ships and freighters in the bay. Yet, I had to stop my car at the entrance of the draw-bridge because the span in the middle was drawn upright to allow ships to pass through underneath. Except they couldn't move.

Well this is stupid, I reacted at first. Then, inspiration struck. I realized that a lot of inefficiency at work might come from routines that aren't applicable every single day. Just as it didn't make sense to pull up the bridge when the boats were frozen, many of our routines don't make sense in every situation. But we keep using them. Maybe my employees would be happier if I studied which steps could be skipped under specific conditions. Suddenly, being delayed in a nonsense drawbridge routine helped me illuminate a solution to workplace productivity problems. If I hadn't been open to inspiration at every opportunity, I might not have realized that efficient routines can sometimes lead to instances of inefficiency. The drawbridge lowered and I continued on my way with a new idea in the back of my head that I could use the next time I needed to problem solve work routine challenges.

Inspiration can arise from literally anywhere. A drawbridge, the people in your corner, the letters in your alphabet soup, even a black hole. Just look around you! Virtually every man-made object in sight once existed in someone's Imagination. Then, they outlined a plan and carried it out to bring this thing into existence. If you're reading this on a tablet or laptop, the technology that makes it possible used to be a dream. If you're reading a physical copy, think of the centuries of ideation it took to develop the first printing press, and then evolve that into the publishing house that allows books like this to be available for thousands of readers. Prior to these inventions, who would have thought any of this would be possible? Realize that life-changing ideas could be in anyone's head, so look beyond yourself to access them. Be receptive to anything, as outlandish or unassuming as it might be. This isn't the time for judging ideas yet. Amass as many options as you can. The solution to your greatest challenge might be a drawbridge away.

4. Turn Dreams Into Visions of Personal or Professional Progress

What's the difference between a dream and vision? A dream is intangible, easily forgotten, and not necessarily realistic. A vision, however, is visible with the naked eye, ever present, and based in a realistic outcome. Visions can start off as dreams, but converting a dream into a vision begins with identifying the dream you wish to realize.

Perhaps you want to send your kid to college, put a down payment on your first home, or get into a competitive program like a sports league or training seminar. You haven't figured out how to attain these goals, but the thought of getting there one day fills you with determination. Use that energy to motivate you to make progress toward your goal. And the best way to make progress is to convert your dream into a vision.

You can turn your dreams into visions for the future by getting as specific, concrete, and granular as possible. Wanting a vacation home by the beach is a dream, but looking up the house you want, researching the price, making a savings plan, and printing out a photo of the property to look at every day makes it a vision. The photo on the wall is a real, tangible thing. It is not a dream, it's a possibility. You've mapped out the path to realize it.

If you don't commit to a dream, it won't become a vision. Commitment means thinking about it every day so you are mindful of which actions lead you closer to your goal and which pull you off track. Your short term actions should drive progress towards a long term vision. You should be on the path to your dreams. Further, you can adjust your path in the face of unexpected challenges. Rather than changing your dream or giving up when the going gets tough, committing to a specific vision puts you in a mindset of progress.

Dreams and visions are similar in one way, they can both be highly ambitious. However, dreams aren't always based on realistic expectations and can lead you into the Despair trap when you fall short of them or can't define exactly what they are. Healthy ambitions, on the other hand, are well-researched and attainable no matter how lofty they might appear. If you have a step-by-step approach to realize a well-defined vision, you will have direction and purpose in your mission and in your life.

The people in your corner should be ambitious visionaries too. When they can see your vision and your passion for personal or professional progress with their own eyes, they'll want to collaborate with you to realize it.

Don't let dreams be dreams, but transform them to visions and envision exactly what you want, then set out to make it happen.

5. Respectfully Challenge Your Cabinet as They Challenge You (...on the edge of discomfort)

After committing to a dream and making it your vision, you need the right people in your corner to help you monitor your progress and keep your Imagination open. Being in an echo chamber is a recipe for disaster as it restricts your Imagination to a narrow range of actions. Unless you invite alternative perspectives, meeting with your cabinet will only feed your ego, set up unrealistic expectations, and cause you to fall right into the traps. If you fail to see problems with your approach, you'll fail to see ways to adjust your trajectory. Your Imagination ought to be challenged so you can consistently come up with creative ways to overcome blindspots and setbacks on your road to achievement.

To assemble team members who will challenge you, avoid people who are nice. I'm not saying you should share your personal and professional ideas with bullies. But, nice people certainly aren't ideal because they will avoid saying anything that might make you uncomfortable, even if it's what you need to hear. You wouldn't ask your sweet grandmother whether a dress looks good on you because you know she'd probably say you look absolutely wonderful, even if she thinks you look like a sail. Her compliment isn't helping anybody and might skew your evaluations rather than correct them.

Instead you want cabinet members who are kind. A kind person would say, *I don't think that dress does you justice. Maybe try this one.* A kind person pushes you towards the edge of discomfort and away from the traps. They'll tell you the truth even when it's not what you want to hear, but they have the decency not to insult you either. A kind teammate challenges you to step up and make personal and professional progress. Likewise, you should kindly challenge your cabinet members so they can stay on the Track of Humility as they move toward their goals.

However, it's not always easy to deliver uncomfortable news in a kind way. That's where practicing these techniques plays a major role. A healthy Imagination will lead to new and creative ways of effectively challenging people to help them get where they need to go. For example, you might consider challenging your cabinet members to take Step Zero on their own. Inspire them to be calm, to compartmentalize, and to get to a blank slate to do their own imaginative thinking.

For example, if you want to help someone calm down, you can get creative in your approach. Blurting out "Just calm down!" almost never works. A more effective strategy might be to ask them if their Imagination is running too fast, which is leading to anxiety about the future. To help them, ask what they fear the worst case scenario might be. Once they say it out loud, they'll probably feel that the worst case scenario isn't all that bad, or at least extremely unlikely. From a calmer temperament, they can better plan for exactly where they want to go.

Imagination plays a role in deciding how to approach the people in your corner. If the people in your corner resist constructive criticism, seriously ask yourself whether the individuals you've selected are aligned with your long term goals, or if they are more for your present convenience. If the answer is 'convenience,' then move on to selecting a new cabinet. People who refuse to grow are not the right people to help you advance toward your personal and professional goals.

It's ideal to surround yourself with people who will respectfully challenge you, keep you on the edge of discomfort, provide moral support, and push you towards self-improvement. Likewise, you want to challenge others to make sure they aren't headed into any of the pitfalls. If they're acting out of selfishness, low self-esteem, or other signs of the Dark, Negative Attitude, you can help them recognize their hindered progress and encourage them to stay on the Track of Humility.

6. Redefine Fear

Through understanding and awareness, you can convert fear into something positive and productive.

We do not fear the past or the present, only the future. Try to think about something you used to fear or currently fear and you'll see it is impossible. We can be depressed about the past, or in emotional distress during the present, but fear and anxiety only occur when we imagine events that haven't happened yet. We can be afraid of disappointing someone we care for, or losing our job, or getting rejected, but as soon as we come face-to-face with these undesirable situations, we are no longer afraid of them. Fear of disappointment becomes actual disappointment when we let someone down. Fear of losing our job transforms to emptiness or frustration when we're fired. Fear of getting rejected can become dejection or self-pity when our crush tells us they're not interested. As soon as something occurs the fear is gone because the object of our fear is no longer in the future. It already happened. We might be afraid about what's going to happen next, but we will not fear what is happening or has happened. Therefore, fear only exists in the future, and because it only exists in the future, it involves our imagination.

To conceive of what's going to happen next, we must use our Imagination. Thus, all fear is based on imagining an undesirable outcome. It's natural to be afraid. In fact, the fear response is one of the most primal, ancient, and useful parts of our biology. It allows us to think about what could go wrong so we can avoid harm. It keeps us away from sheer cliffs, predatory animals, and embarrassing social situations. We experience anxiety at every challenge before us as an instinctual defense mechanism. While this can be helpful in certain situations, unchecked fear can be a huge distraction from pursuing our goals.

Imagining the worst can cause us to freeze up and avoid taking the next step forward. It might trigger immense self-doubt that pulls us onto the negative emotional track and into the pitfall of Despair. Fear might influence our thinking so that we start to overvalue potential negative outcomes and under-value positive ones before we make a decision. However, it's possible to derive power from fear and use it to fuel your next greatest accomplishment.

The first step in redefining fear is to imagine the worst case scenario. For instance, maybe I'm anxious about meeting my sales quota this month because if I fall short I'll make less money, and if I make less money, I'll struggle to cover my next house payment. As soon as I imagine missing a home payment, a whole new cycle of fear begins. It's not a pretty picture, but worrying about it is distracting me from doing what I need to do: make sales.

I have to realize that this fear, no matter how vivid, isn't going to kill me. If my imagination has me sleeping in my car, or spending the night on my friend's floor, or even curling up outside in the cold, I can think about all the times I've actually done those things! I've slept in my car on road trips, crashed at my friends' places before, and I've endured freezing nights in the woods camping on multiple occasions The embarrassment of losing my house might be concerning, but I know I can always bounce back, get support if I need it, and find a way to get a roof over my head again. I can live with sleeping in the car. However, it's not ideal. So, once I've accepted the worst possible outcome, I can start working out how to avoid it.

I need to use my Imagination to develop a positive source of motivation rather than a negative one. Instead of operating from a place of fear, I can operate with determination inspired by opportunity. I can meet my quota because I want to be a great salesman. I remind myself that I took this job to learn how to sell cars like the best of them. I want to achieve my vision of professionalism. If my biggest fear is taking a blow to my ego through failure, my greatest desire is to prove that I am capable of accomplishing my goal.

If I accept that the worst case scenario isn't too much for me to handle, I can put that worry aside and focus instead on imagining a path to achieve my vision and carrying it out to the best of my abilities. It will cement my confidence to set reasonable expectations for myself and do the work required to realize my goals, even if that means learning new skills. Without fear distracting my Imagination, I can propel myself towards my goal more effectively. By training my Imagination, I can convert my fear of failure into motivation for progress.

A World of Your Imagination

Cultivating your Imagination will lead to greater visions of success and more ways to realize them. Anything you want to do, do it. Want to change the world? There's nothing to it. Just ask how? Why? And then who?

First, stimulate your inner dialogue by taking a judgment-free approach to creative thinking. Entertain any and all ideas to make sure no stone is unturned nor pathway unexplored.

Next, don't go with your gut. Temper your confidence in your ability to choose the best plan of action based on prior successes and failures. It's critical to evaluate every challenge as an independent scenario so you can ask the right questions to achieve success. If you rest on your laurels, overconfidence might lead you off the Track of Humility.

Judgment-free and humbled, look beyond yourself to find other sources of inspiration for creative thinking. The answer you need could come from a conversation with a friend, an inquiry on the Internet, or watching the leaves fall. You never know when inspiration might strike, so it's imperative to keep an open mind to anything that might stir your Imagination.

Having considered every possible future scenario, fixate on your vision for personal and professional progress. Where do you see yourself? What do you want? Take that dream and convert it into a tangible vision. Use your Imagination to devise a route to realize your vision and be sure to sample your progress often to ensure you're on the right track, adjusting when necessary.

On your path to achieving your goals, utilize the people in your corner to challenge you and keep you out of the traps. Likewise, challenge your cabinet to make sure they're staying on the Track of Humility. It takes creative solutions to kindly challenge each other and walk on the edge of discomfort as you pursue your vision.

Finally, take all of your fears and bring them to the surface. See them for the personalized emotional blackmail that they are, and take away their power. Imagine the worst case scenario and accept that it might happen, but won't be as terrible as you think. Consider how many times in the past you have been afraid. How many of your imagined fears came to life? (If I'm giving you the benefit of the doubt, my guess is less than 5%.) Take the power away from your fear and replace it with the power of positive motivation.

If you feel that fear motivates you more than opportunity, consider why you are focusing on the negative. You may accomplish your goal, but at the same time that negative energy will drain you and the people you are close to in the long run.

Realizing your dream could be wonderful, like signing the deed on that new vacation house by the beach. But some dreams are nightmares. Without a healthy value system, you might use the power of your Imagination to re-alize a terrible vision, like getting revenge on your neighbor. While you might use Imagination to accomplish this type of goal, it won't help you develop professionally or personally. Therefore, we need to utilize Values, the Second Element, to keep ourselves on track...

Chapter 7
Values

To develop profound foresight it isn't enough to simply stay on the Track of Humility and avoid the pitfalls, we must also utilize the Elements of Imagination, Values, and Efficiency. The symbiotic relationship between these three intersecting components will allow us to experience a vision beyond the moment. These Elements work together in a sequence but they also build on each other in a cyclical fashion.

Imagination is the first phase, when you explore every idea you can in all extremes. No judgment or bias should be present. Next, your Values come into play, allowing you to clean up your thoughts and center yourself emotionally. Efficiency, the final phase, is about the productive use of your cleaned-up thoughts. In this chapter we'll review Values, the second of the three Elements for developing foresight. You'll see why the right types of Values are so important in helping you develop a vision beyond the present moment.

Mastering the Element of Values means practicing actions that reflect healthy Values, especially when you are alone. Your character is revealed by your behavior when no one is looking. All Values boil down to two types: light side values and dark side values.

Respect, Generosity, Trust, and Empathic Listening are a few of the many positive Values we can cultivate. Likewise, Vengeance, Selfishness, Arrogance, and Reactive Listening are examples of dark side Values. Light side and dark side Values are easily identifiable because they align with our internal concept of right and wrong. Our goal will not be to eliminate dark sided thoughts entirely, but to learn how to pause them, challenge them, and convert them into strengths.

When we discussed the Three Misalignments we noted that actions spawning from the Dark, Negative Attitude are a result of our misaligned internal value system. This misalignment makes us uncomfortable and that discomfort can cause us to act impulsively. We distort reality to deflect what is emotionally overwhelming. That's not emotionally productive.

We all know when we have done something wrong, such as stealing, cheating, or gossiping. Yet many of us continue to work against our own value system. Why do we fall off the Track of Humility and embrace a Dark, Negative spiral when we clearly know the difference between right and wrong? Why do we sacrifice our Values and continue to lie, cheat, or steal even when we know it's wrong?

We work against our value system because we are impulsive and emotional. For instance, we might lie because we are afraid that someone won't accept us if they knew the truth. We may steal out of fear that we'll starve if we don't. Or out of anger toward those who have more than us. We get onto an emotional track that pulls us into acting against our Values. Then we justify our behavior to make ourselves feel better.

Learning to control our impulses is the most crucial step in the self development process. Controlling our behavior and refraining from making a decision on the spot will allow us to better understand what is going on within us, as well as what is going on around us that is pulling us off the Track of Humility.

Emotional Impulses

David and Sue are an unlikely couple who have been dating for a few months. David is a professional. He goes to work on time and deals with non-profits that reflect his internal value system. He has to make certain sacrifices to make time for his son, and now Sue also, but he takes personal responsibility for making those relationships as strong as possible. He is open to feedback, which he takes as an opportunity to improve and better contribute to his relationships.

Sue loves to have fun. She's excited to go out to happy hour three nights per week, and is open to whatever the night has in store. She'll travel on a whim, seizing the day but skimping on the logistics. And she doesn't hold herself back from inviting other men to party with her, even though she's in a relationship with David.

In this example, Sue isn't deeply connecting with what is important to David. Sue will justify her behavior with, "David isn't as outgoing as I wish," or, "These guys are just friends," and, "I stayed home all week so what's a little fun anyways?" These excuses are a way of justifying behavior that isn't in line with her Values. It is in the space between our internal Values and external behaviors that many of us begin to lie, deflect, and deny the reality of what we are doing.

David is putting his foot forward to try and make it work, but something is wrong. A knot forms in his stomach every time she doesn't answer her phone. *I was just out with the girls… My phone was off…* He knows something is going on.

The problem here is a misalignment of core Values between David and Sue as a result of impulsive behavior and a difference in their priorities. Sue trusts David because he's respectful, caring, and reliable, but David doesn't trust Sue because she's impulsive and cannot live up to her verbal promises. David doesn't respect Sue's behavior or her frivolous lifestyle, but he works on staying with her because he's operating impulsively due to the guilt of breaking a commitment, and he enjoys being with her when they do get along.

Sue is drawn to David, but follows her impulse to keep the party going instead of ending or improving the relationship. She sees the convenience and security of having a responsible partner. He represents what her idealistic view of life is, and she hopes to eventually live up to that sense of responsibility… one day. They both enjoy having fun together, but they are not practicing important Values such as Trust and Respect. Their emotional impulses cause them both to act in ways that are inconsistent with their Values. David impulsively lies to himself, acting as if Sue will change because he's making sacrifices for the relationship. Sue impulsively overestimates David, thinking he will magically change into a more carefree person. Neither of them are going to change, but their egos both think they are special enough that the other will change for them.

To overcome our impulses, we need to increase our emotional awareness and connect to our value system. We are naturally attracted to connections with people whose Values align with our own. When we can't find that, we distort our own Values and those of the people around us to fool ourselves into thinking we are in alignment. It's another way our subconscious attempts to fill the void. Understanding this tendency will help us become more aware of when we are lying to ourselves, like David and Sue were.

The key to cultivating relationships in which our values are truly aligned with the other person's is to develop a Bright, Positive Attitude. David and Sue need to resist the distortions of the Dark, Negative Attitude and gain control over their impulses so they can connect with their true Values. They can have an open conversation about how their Values are misaligned and decide to either be more open with each other, go their separate ways so they can both live better lives, or come up with some other plan to ensure they're always reflecting Love, Trust, and Respect.

Behaving in ways that reflect your true Values will allow you to feel good about yourself, and over time it will become a habit. Your external behaviors will gradually align more closely with your internal value system, and you will no longer impulsively work against yourself. It isn't easy to confront our distortions and admit we have strayed away from our true Values, but it's the first step toward living a life of true alignment. The more time we spend in alignment, the more we feel accomplished and proud of the decisions we make as a whole. This makes it easier to avoid the Dark, Negative Attitude and stay on the Track of Humility the next time around.

Make Every Second Count

What do the following numbers all have in common?

31,536,000

525,600

8,760

365

52

12

1

They probably look familiar, especially the latter ones. These numbers all represent the same period of time.

1 Year is the same as:

12 Months

52 Weeks

365 Days

8,760 Hours

525,600 Minutes or

31,536,000 Seconds

That's 31,536,000 opportunities to realign yourself with your true Values this year alone. And you can choose to start this second!

The longer you work against your Values, the further down you'll go down the wrong track. Remember, the distance you travel in the wrong direction is equal to the distance you'll have to backtrack to return to ground zero. Seconds will add up to hours, days, weeks, months, and years. Suddenly you'll find yourself ten years down a track that doesn't reflect your value system. You could be married to the wrong person, working in the wrong career, or hanging out with the wrong crowd.

When you look back at the last 10 years, remember it started 315,359,999 seconds ago. If you didn't have the foresight to develop a realistic plan to obtain your goals, then you probably didn't achieve many of them. And if you did get the things you wanted, the success may have excited you and pulled you off the Track of Humility and out of alignment with your Values.

Do you want to wake up one day thinking, "I wish I would've done it another way," or do you want to be thinking, "I'm glad I didn't do it any other way"? Trying to rehash what you could have done differently is a form of living in the past. This is where you begin reminisce, and a regretful doom loop starts to spin, pulling you into the Dark, Negative Attitude where you feel a growing sense of resentment for yourself, your position, your choices, and the other people who have done you wrong. As the doom loop spins faster you'll unleash and expose the nasty side of yourself. The farther you journey down this negative emotional track the harder it is to return to neutral.

So if you're like David, or Sue, or somewhere in between, don't waste another second living a life in which your thoughts and actions don't align with your long term view of the future. It will erode your self-esteem, bring out your Dark, Negative Attitude, and drive your relationships and aspirations into the ground. You'll bite your tongue until you have no tongue left at all. This is how you end up alive without a spark of life in you.

If you are walking the planet without life in you, it's time to change this very second. Forgive yourself for falling into whatever pitfall is holding you hostage, and forgive others around you who are trapped in pitfalls of their own. Forgiveness is not about letting an injustice off of the hook. Forgiveness actually has less to do with the past and more to do with the present. It is about creating space within ourselves for a more healthy mental state. It's about opening our eyes to future opportunities instead of rehashing the past in our head, wishing we could go back and have a redo. If you're struggling with forgiveness because a person who harmed you is still in your life and you cannot walk away, you are in a challenging situation. You must forgive while also establishing a boundary.

Save yourself the emotional weight and start aligning your Values with your actions now. Don't waste another second. You already know what to do. Your value system is easily identifiable because you know the difference between right and wrong. If you need any help identifying your true Values, ask the people in your corner to help.

Give yourself a real, unflinching test to see if you're living in accordance with your value system. Ask, "How do I feel about the person I have become?" and you'll know whether you're making the right actions. Commit to positive behaviors, reap the rewards, and feel good about living in alignment with your true self. As you grow more connected to your value system, you'll learn to make decisions that keep you out of the Dark, Negative Attitude.

To master your Values, there are six steps you can take to control your impulses, align your actions, and ultimately feel whole with everything you do.

But before we can take the first step to become emotionally productive, we must learn how to overcome emotional blackmail and insecurities. To master the Element of Values, this is Step Zero.

Step Zero – Overcome Emotional Blackmail

Emotional blackmail is when we value our reputation more highly than we value actually acting in alignment with our inner moral compass. We begin to protect a romanticized view of ourselves and we cling to that image because we feel that if the truth was exposed we would experience guilt and shame. Fearing these feelings makes us uncomfortable, which pushes us even farther down the negative emotional track and out of alignment. Instead of facing the discomfort, analyzing our Values, and getting back to neutral, we continue compensating to protect the illusion.

It's like the high schooler who doesn't make the team, so he tells everyone he didn't really want to play soccer anyway. He's afraid to tell others how much the sport means to him and face the feelings of rejection, so he pretends he doesn't care. To protect this illusion he stops practicing and he stops watching soccer on TV. As time goes on he slides farther out of alignment with his true Values.

When we experience emotional blackmail, we hold ourselves emotionally hostage, maintaining this idealized state of denial to avoid the difficult emotions, fearing we won't know how to manage them. Instead of making progress, we remain in suspense. The emotional blackmail that we impose on ourselves is astronomically damaging because in an attempt to drown out our insecurities, we taint the parts of ourselves that we are comfortable with.

When sticking with a healthy diet, for example, we at times fixate on our insecurities in an attempt to motivate ourselves. But it doesn't work for long. We go right back to the previous diet a few weeks later, resulting in guilt. These shameful feelings open the door for emotional blackmail to grab hold of us and corrupt our best qualities. We allow our insecurities to dominate our attitude, pushing us further down a path that ends in despair. Maybe we start to joke about our love handles, take pride in our ability to eat anything, and make fun of healthy people to protect the image that we are happy with our body.

To combat emotional blackmail, use the Naked Mirror Test. The Naked Mirror Test, referenced in the last chapter, can also help resolve emotional blackmail. Strip down and look at yourself in the mirror. Then, go through a list of your attributes, both physical and nonphysical, and recite how you feel about each one. Say to yourself.

- I feel _____ about my hips.
- I feel _____ about my weight.
- I feel _____ about my eye and hair color.
- I feel _____ about my ability to learn new things.
- I feel _____ about my social relationships.
- I feel _____ about my level of extroversion.
- I feel _____ about my level of ambition.
- I feel _____ about my current level of education.
- I feel _____ about my overall attitude toward people.

Go beyond these examples and do this exercise for any traits that are important or emotional for you.

Score yourself on each attribute on from 1-10, with 1 being a low score and 10 being a high score. For some attributes you'll score highly. Your greatest strengths are probably 9s and 10s. For other attributes, you'll score near the bottom. If you feel that your level extroversion only scores a 2, then you have to accept that you're not an extroverted person. That's natural for you and you shouldn't bully yourself, feel guilty, or otherwise emotionally blackmail yourself when you receive a low score. Become comfortable with that 2 and embrace that it's a part who you are right now.

When you gain comfort with an insecurity it loses potency. On the other hand, being uncomfortable with something gives it power. Things that make us feel bad are tagged as threats in our brain. We think about them constantly and we end up with a knot in our stomach. Instead of accepting our shortcoming and letting it go, we keep it around so it can haunt us and inhibit our emotional productivity.

The goal of Step Zero is not to ignore what makes us insecure, but to embrace our insecurities and become comfortable in who we are. Look that insecurity in the face instead of trying to erase it or pretend it doesn't exist. You won't get anywhere ignoring it and hoping it goes away on its own. Insecurities will only grow stronger until you accept them. If you feel insecure about your health you can become more secure by acknowledging specifically what it is about your health you want to change. Then use your Imagination to come up with some potential ways to adjust your self-care habits and put yourself on the path to your goals.

Of course, we can't change all objects of our insecurity. If you feel insecure about something you are stuck with, like your height or your family, learn to accept it in a way that will remove the emotional blackmail. Don't deny its existence, because that allows the insecurity and emotional blackmail to continue wreaking havoc on your growth.

It's important to uncover why we feel insecure about certain things. Then we can make a list of which attributes are changeable and which are not and plan to change what we can. When we understand what is within our control and what is out of our hands, we can direct our focus to taking responsibility for who we are. With a sense of responsibility, we will no longer emotionally blackmail ourselves with insecurity. We will say, "This is who I am and I'm okay with that."

Taking personal responsibility for your life is required for this chapter on Values to be most effective. If we can't take responsibility for everything we feel secure and insecure about, we can't be emotionally productive. So before we move onto Step One, we have to become comfortable with acknowledging how we truthfully feel about ourselves. The good, bad, and ugly.

1. Practicing Generosity, Self-Respect, Respect of Others, and Honor

To become emotionally productive and beat impulses, you must acknowledge your true inner Values and begin to live in accordance with them. The four cornerstone Values of Generosity, Self-Respect, Respect of Others, and Honor are a great starting point. While Values are personal and everyone's are slightly different, I've found these four to be universal.

Generosity

Operating with generosity means giving a meaningful portion of what you have to someone in need. This can be anything from time to knowledge to money, and it can be given anonymously or publicly. If you don't have a penny to your name, you can give your time and effort. Time holds value for everyone, so donating your time to help others is always a generous gesture. If you have a million dollars in the bank, you can offer a comfortable amount of money as part of your action plan to be generous to someone in need.

I refer to generosity as a cornerstone value because I've found that if you truly become generous in your actions to others and to yourself, the rest will fall in order. My dear friend Neil says the way you do the littlest things in life is how you do the biggest things. There isn't a separation. Life is all encompassing. So be generous, even if it feels like you don't have anything to give. Align your actions with this value now.

Self-Respect

Practicing the value of self-respect means doing the right thing when no one is looking. When the only person you can let down is yourself, do you underperform? Do you cut corners? Do you work too hard and burn yourself out? Analyze how much respect and dignity you have for yourself.

When you cultivate self-respect and raise your internal standards, you won't allow yourself to slack off or watch opportunities pass you by. You'll be motivated to achieve your goals independently because your high standards will naturally inspire you to take the steps needed for completion. Continue to ask yourself every day whether you're making decisions that are aligned with the value of self-respect, and correct yourself when you veer off track.

Don't buy into your own excuses, as they are symptoms of emotional blackmail. Sometimes it's more respectful to be hard on ourselves than it is to let ourselves off the hook. Have the self-respect to look critically at your own behavior and analyze where you have fallen short. But don't let your past mistakes and their consequences ruin your confidence. Don't let insecurities arise within you and create emotional blackmail. Strive to always do the things you know you should do. This is a sign of the amount of respect you have for yourself.

Respect of Others

When you have respect for others it means you won't take advantage of people or systems. For example, if you were sitting next to a blind man who had a $100 bill in front of him, would you slip a $1 bill into its place and take the $100 bill knowing he wouldn't be able to tell the difference? This is an obvious answer for most people. But what if you were faced with a scenario where you were selling a product—say a car or a home—and you knew something was wrong but the other party didn't notice the issue? Unfortunately this is also an obvious answer for most people. The majority of us would choose to remain silent. This is why these types of larger transactions tend to have disclosure statements.

When you choose to not make others aware of meaningful information that you are aware of, you are taking from the blind.

For a more typical example, imagine you're at the grocery store and the clerk forgets to ring up one of your items. You could take advantage of the employee and the store. You could get a free item and no one would be the wiser. However, getting away with theft by passing it off as a mistake doesn't align with your Values. You know it's wrong. To do what's right, remind yourself to respect the employee by letting her know she made a mistake so she can do her job correctly. Respect the store by taking responsibility for your role as a customer and paying for everything you intend to take home.

Honor

Cultivating honor means being respectful to the overarching environment and system that you are a part of. This goes beyond you and the people around you. Honor is about protecting the commitments made to a cause. This involves marriage, parenthood, your chosen religion, a person's privacy, promises, your relationship with your employer, and any other regimens you are committed too. In the end it requires discipline to follow through in spite of how you feel at any given moment.

For example, if you see a man on the street drop a twenty dollar bill you have the option to act honorably and return the dropped money. Or you could dishonor the universal law of "don't take what doesn't belong to you" by pocketing the twenty.

Likewise, if you are required to punch in and out for lunch breaks at work, it would be honorable to record your breaks with accuracy, but unjust to take advantage of the system by stretching the boundaries of breaktime in your favor, especially when no one is looking or monitoring.

And if you hear gossip, it would be dishonorable to jump on the bandwagon and spread rumors impulsively. Whereas, it's just to say, "That person is not here right now, how about we hold off on this conversation until we get their side of the story." Further, being honorable means not being the first to talk poorly about family members or co-workers behind their backs. Even if we are sure we know the whole story, it isn't ours to tell. Opening our mouth would be bearing false witness against a neighbor. The only benefit of gossip is that it can sooth your insecurity in the moment. But this comes at the expense of your honor. Is it really worth it?

If you're behaving in a way that is not honorable, respectful of others, respectful of yourself, or generous, then you know exactly where to start getting into alignment. Practice these four Values to overcome impulsiveness and increase the alignment of your value system. Commit to never speaking poorly of others or taking advantage of the system. You have 31,536,000 seconds until next year, grab the nearest one and say, "This starts right now."

2. Do Not Transfer Blame

The second step to mastering the Element of Values is to start taking responsibility instead of transferring blame. Taking responsibility is relevant for every aspect of developing foresight. Wherever you are in life, you are responsible for fulfilling a role. You might be a parent, a teacher, an employer, some combination of the three, or something else entirely. Whatever your role, you have a duty to fulfill it.

When things don't go as planned, it's easy to point your finger at another person. If I didn't make the mark at work, I might blame my boss. If someone didn't want to go out on a date with me, she must be crazy. If I'm unhappy, it's not my fault. We make excuses and avoid responsibility to protect our grandiose vision of ourselves. We don't want to admit we aren't as great as we thought, and our insecurities prevent us from accurately evaluating our situation and taking responsibility for being there. Overall, transferring blame works against our value system.

To control the emotional impulse to deflect blame, we have to remind ourselves that our situation is always 110% our own fault. We must recognize that the position we're in right now is a culmination of our choices. At first, it is very difficult to accept total responsibility. If someone wrongs you, isn't it their fault you feel bad, not your own? No. You are in control of your internal state. If you feel negatively about yourself or about someone else, you are the only one responsible for feeling that way.

If there's a feeling you don't like, take responsibility for changing it. If you deflect, transfer, or ignore responsibility for feeling down, you're missing an opportunity to take matters into your own hands and improve the situation. Instead of feeling bad about where you are, take responsibility to improve it.

One way to execute this is to build a road map to take you from a situation you don't like to one you do like. Maybe you want to change the balance in your bank account, the way your kids behave, or the number of hours you dedicate to sleeping. Take responsibility and make a game plan to improve the areas of your life that you don't like. If you don't know how to get started, ask the people in your corner to help out. If you don't have anyone in your corner with credentials suitable for planning out your road map, try to find someone who is in the position you aim to be in and interview them for advice on how to get there. As a last resort, you can look at Youtube for editorials and educational videos aligned to the subject at hand.

The best time to start taking responsibility is this very second. Turn your feet in a new direction and begin to walk down a path of emotional productivity. Pledge to take responsibility for all new and unforeseen challenges. Decide that you will do the work necessary to overcome them. With the guidance of your cabinet, look for ways to improve by taking matters into your own hands.

Taking responsibility and independently solving problems is emotionally productive because it builds on your self confidence and strengthens your character. With each challenge faced, you'll be rewarded with experience and wisdom to better prepare for what's next. Instead of transferring blame, embrace failure as an opportunity for self-growth. Fight blame-game impulses and work to take full control of your choices in life.

3. The Right Things, the Right Way, for the Right Reasons

Doing the right things, the right way, for the right reasons, also known as the Three R's, is the third step in developing Values. Following the Three R's is only possible when you have good intentions for your actions. Sometimes you can do the right thing for the wrong reason, such as donating to charity just to get attention. While being generous is generally a good thing, donating for a selfish reason is not in line with a healthy value system.

When faced with a challenge, especially a time sensitive one, we often have the impulse to get ahead by cheating or stealing. We might want to take a gamble without doing the proper research, leading us to take irrational risks. When we act this way, we are aiming to complete our goal by any means necessary, rather than by the best means possible. From this frame of mind, cheating sounds like a good option. But to maintain a healthy value system you must choose the right options with the right intentions and carry them out in the right ways. A large part of this is performing due diligence and removing your emotional attachment to how you think things "should" be.

An attorney once told me that we can never do enough due diligence, and it's some of the best advice I've ever heard. Take buying a home for example. If you're buying a home for yourself or your family, you want it to be perfect. This is where you're going to spend the majority of your time and it's a big financial investment. When it comes to buying property, the last thing you want is to get cheated. You want to fully understand what you're getting into, what's involved with maintaining the house, who built the house, and what materials they built it out of. You want to know about the neighbors and the history, the local tax codes, the public works, and anything else that might be important.

You would do the same if you were buying a new business. You would want to know about the employees, bureaucracy, and nepotism. What does the culture look like? Does every person cover their own self-interest, or do people act with a greater vision for the organization? Who started the company and why? What are the Values of the company and the mission? Make sure the customers are always the focal point, or the business won't last. Similarly, in a school, make sure the students are the focal point, not the faculty. And be sure your mayor's focal point is helping the community, not getting reelected. A vision beyond the moment is a crucial element of long term success.

Performing the necessary due diligence means doing enough research to know that you're getting involved in the right things, the right way, for the right reasons. If you follow your impulses and get involved with the wrong crowd, career, or car choices, you'll end up regretting it. Or worse, you'll convince yourself you don't regret it and become a charlatan. The Three R's are a great way to check in on your decisions and make sure your actions are in line with your value system. Consistently implementing the Three R's will keep you on the Track of Humility as you master Values.

4. Understanding Others Requires Empathetic Listening

To further align your value system, avoid the impulse to jump to conclusions. Instead, listen empathically. As every person is different, the same message can reach people in a variety of ways. To ensure you're talking with someone in a way that they understand, you must first learn to understand them through empathic listening. This means listening with your heart, and not just your ears. Absorb more than just the facts. Focus on perceiving someone's personality, how they feel, where they're coming from, how they see the world, and ultimately what their desires are.

Empathetic listening means having an open ear, an open mind, and a blank slate to let in fresh information that you can respond to, rather than react to. Don't jump to conclusions about where someone is coming from before you hear them out. To be an effective listener and communicator, try to avoid thinking, "How can I get my point across?" because that's a selfish mindset.

To really understand others, you should ask instead, "How does this person see the situation? What value do they place on what we're about to discuss? How can I be considerate of them, but also provide something of value to them? How will this information relate to their life?" Operating with this mindset introduces empathy and reminds you to listen before speaking. It shifts your focus away from the information you want to say and gets you thinking instead about what people need to hear. Fight the impulse of assuming you know what's best for someone. You really don't know where they're coming from. It's more emotionally productive to listen with empathy before trying to understand someone, and to understand before you attempt to communicate your own message.

5. Respond Instead of React

The difference between responding and reacting can be illustrated by thinking about a medication. If a rash were to appear on your arm, you'd want to deal with it so it stops bothering you. The rash could respond to a topical medication, meaning it goes away with treatment. Or, it could react to the medication, causing more irritation. Responding means the problem goes away, while reacting means it gets worse.

In communication, reactions are impulsive and tend to escalate issues rather than resolve them. As mentioned in step four, If you try to communicate with someone without empathically hearing them, you won't be able to accurately help them. However, if you can listen to their issue in its entirety without cutting them off, filling in the blanks, or forcing a certain answer, you'll be able to respond more carefully and address the problem.

Being patient and understanding demonstrates alignment with the Values of caring and assistance. Listening deeply is the best way to make huge strides towards solving a problem. Next, respond with the best resources you have available, and if someone needs something that is beyond your skill set, you can say, "I really don't know enough about this subject to be the best help to you." It's okay not to have the answer as long as you can be supportive and admit when you aren't the expert someone needs.

Other times, people don't want advice, they just want to emotionally unload. Don't make the mistake of offering advice to people who aren't receptive to it. Instead of reacting to someone's problem by immediately explaining what you would do, listen carefully to see if they are truly looking for advice. If it sounds like they only want to vent, find a way to respond without telling them what to do.

Remembering to respond instead of react allows us to address others' problems without being impulsive. We need to slow down and take the next step that will move us toward a solution rather than going with our gut and doing whatever feels right in the moment.

6. Problem Solving is More Important Than Being Right

The sixth step in training the Element of Values is to recognize that you don't always need to be right to solve problems. Staying productive means choosing your battles carefully. Sometimes the best way to get something done is to hold your tongue.

Imagine you're in a room with 10 other people when someone begins to describe how to play a certain card game. You recognize this game. You're not just familiar with it, you know the game from childhood and you understand the rules like the back of your hand. You notice that in explaining the game, this person has left out a few details. Knowing these minute rules won't make a difference among this group of newcomers to the game, but you could interrupt and explain the proper rules anyway. Should you do it?

If you were to interrupt the game, you would be proving a point at no gain to the other players, but at the expense of embarrassing the person trying to explain the rules. The only gain would be your sense of being right. It's tempting to speak up when you have the opportunity to make a point, but it's not always necessary. We ought to slow down and ask ourselves if we are doing it for the purpose of helping the cause or just to inflate our ego. Picking fights to be right instead of to solve problems is a sign of the Grandiose Mindset.

To cultivate positive Values, try to see yourself as part of a bigger picture. Skip being right and instead respond in a way that's helpful for everyone else involved. Sometimes doing the right thing means letting someone else be right. Prioritizing helpful solutions over boosting your ego is emotionally productive.

Living With the Values

While these steps are listed from Zero to Six, they are not necessarily chronological. These steps are all intertwined and feed off of each other. The best approach to mastering the Element of Values is to start with the steps you are the best at already and work to improve your ability to practice the others. When you master all the steps, you will have fluidity in your thought process. You will be able to resist prioritizing selfish values over self-improvement values. As you live a life in line with your value system, you'll find many benefits.

When you mastering Values others will want to work more closely with you. Your relationships will become more healthy. And your sense of purpose will be ignited. When you're working to better yourself, people around you will notice and invite you to take more responsibility in their lives as well. You will stop seeing yourself as the center of the universe. Instead, you'll see yourself as a piece of the puzzle, working collaboratively with others to form the bigger picture.

Those who struggle to align their actions with their value system will be continuously pulled off the Track of Humility and into the pitfalls: Grandiosity, Entitlement, Charlatanism, Despair, Excuses, and Discreditable. Each of these Mindsets relates back to shirking responsibility, building up illusions to protect the ego, and shielding our insecurities. At the core of these pitfalls is impulsiveness, the desire to do what our emotions provoke us to do instead of what's best in a situation.

We seek instant gratification in an instant world, taking shortcuts wherever we can to get ahead. This impulsiveness acts like a drug habit. We get addicted to acting emotionally. For this reason, even if we start this second, it can take weeks or years to finally break old habits and replace them with a more positive value system. The sooner we start, though, the sooner we will feel accomplished.

Mastering the Element of Values requires a lifetime of practice. These steps need to be revisited frequently. It's a time-consuming process, but being patient with ourselves and others is worth it. Patience helps us choose emotionally productive steps that align with a healthy value system. In the next chapter, we'll discuss the third and final element, Efficiency. Efficiency makes the journey to our desired outcome more clear and complete.

Chapter 8
Efficiency

This is the final chapter on the three Elements, where we'll take a deep dive into Efficiency by discussing what it's about, how it plays into the other Elements, and why it will take you to your goals on the straightest route feasible.

Efficiency isn't about reaching your goals as fast as humanly possible, it's about slowing down so you don't end up on the wrong path. When you jump to conclusions and take actions that inadvertently lead you away from your goal, you will have to spend more time and energy to get back on track. Accuracy is more efficient.

Take the example of the instruction-following test. In elementary schools, some teachers demonstrate the importance of reading all the instructions before starting the assignment through a phony exam. On the top of the exam, students will find a typical warning message, "Do not start this test without reading all the instructions first." Students who are in a hurry to finish the test as fast as possible will glance over this instruction and start filling out questions. Likewise, students who are overconfident in their ability to ace the test will disregard the instruction and gallivant straight into the test. But the last section of the exam flips the concept of test-taking on its head.

The final instruction on the back of the test reads, "Do not write your name at the top of the exam above question one. Instead, write it here and don't answer any of the questions. For every question completed, you will be docked one point."

Approaching this test with guns-blazing will result in a failing score. Those who read the instructions thoroughly will earn a perfect score. What's intriguing about this test is that the students who write their name on the bottom and turn in an otherwise blank quiz will actually finish faster than those who attempt to work out the problems. By slowing down to read each question before making any progress on answering them, students who followed the rules were more efficient. In this way, Efficiency isn't about doing things as fast as possible. It's about pausing to consider your options before taking action.

When we resist the temptation to get started right away, we can identify the most efficient route forward.

The best way to contemplate your options and consider the next best step is to make sure your head, your heart, and your gut are all in alignment with each other. In other words, you must align your spirit, your impact, and your timing with your environment. Let's explore this.

1. Align Spirit, Impact, and Timing with your Environment

The first step to mastering Efficiency is to align your spirit, impact, and timing with the universe (the environment around you). To align these factors with our current environment, we first need to understand them.

Spirit

Our spirit is the raw emotional energy that shapes our attitude and motivates us to take action. Our spirit wants us to respond to everything right away without thinking twice. Sometimes it reflects our true desires, while other times its impulsiveness can lead us away from our healthy Values. That's why the Spirit must be balanced with Impact and Timing to ensure we slow down and find the next step that best aligns with our Values.

Impact

Impact is how we affect other people. It's the result of our attitude manifesting itself through our actions. Nearly everything we do in life affects another person in some way. A passing comment on the bus could leave a complete stranger's head swimming for the rest of the day. Giving a homeless person twenty dollars might save their life. Even the way we cut our lawn can affect the way everyone in our neighborhood looks. Every decision followed by an action will have an impact on another person in some way. Whatever we do, there is always an effect. This effect could be healthy or unhealthy for others, which is why we need to consider our Impact to ensure we're taking healthy actions.

Timing

Timing can be summed up in one simple phrase: Every second counts. We always have to pay attention to the track we're on by observing our actions and making adjustments when necessary. This means we need to not be the kids on the instruction-following test who jumped in and started solving math problems before finding out we're off track. However, we also must avoid getting locked up with inaction by over evaluating our position and stalling our next move. When we have good Timing we are able to balance these competing energies and move forward at exactly the right moment.

Relation to Environment

If Spirit, Impact, and Timing are three lenses, the Environment is what pulls them into focus. The alignment of these factors depends mostly on the Environment but its complexity makes it difficult to effectively control. Since we can't completely control our environment, we have to align everything else to suit it. Before we can do this, we must perform an accurate assessment of where we are in the universe. Then we must accept the results.

Do a full analysis of what you observe and listen to the truth. Oftentimes we see and hear the truth but choose to ignore it.

What is your position relative to your family and friends? Are your relationships healthy? How about your own health? Do you have your fitness under control or do you have challenges there? Where are you in life, exactly? If you listen to the universe, you can tune into what's going on and use that information to move forward with Efficiency.

Testing Whether You are in Alignment with Your Environment

To know whether you're in accurate alignment with your environment, you need to evaluate your position from a place of centered humility and respect for a higher power. Getting into a neutral mindset and performing a self-check with ourselves in the mirror will help us ask the right questions to discern whether we are in alignment with the environment. If we can ask the right questions, we can encourage ourselves to behave in ways that bring our Spirit, Impact, and Timing into better alignment with the space around us and the people we connect with. We cannot will ourselves to do the right thing without first bringing these four elements into alignment. Failure to do this signals the beginning of the end of any long term relationship or endeavor, because our inner misalignment will drive us off track.

"Mastery of the world is achieved by letting things take their natural course. You can not master the world by changing the natural way." -Lao Tzu.

To perform an accurate analysis of our environment we must learn to listen to our head, heart, and gut. Let's work backwards to understand these three aspects of your analysis, starting with your gut.

Your gut instinct is what you feel you should be doing. It is a rod that connects with your Spirit. Ask yourself whether you're doing what you know is right according to your instinct (your gut). Is your environment suggesting you're headed down the right path, or are you finding yourself in a place that feels disconnected from your expectations? Your gut instinct should be one of harmony with your current environment. If it isn't you should re evaluate your position.

Always check in with your gut, no matter how strong your desire to act is. The more intensely you want to act on instinct, the greater your liability for failures down the road tends to be.

Your heart is the second thing to take into account during your analysis, and it connects to your passions. It also relates to how your actions will affect others through your Impact. Your impact on others will either fuel the fire of your passion, or extinguish it. When you have an authentic connection between heart and Spirit, you lose track of time and find yourself in a state of flow. Energy will flow through you, emanating into your surroundings and positively impacting others around you.

Ask yourself whether your passion aligns with what is healthy for your environment. If not, it will be counterproductive. Ideally, you should wait until the environment is right before you follow your heart and realize your passion. You don't want to buy a stock you love when its price is inflated. In this case, the environment wouldn't be right for you to follow your heart. You must wait until market conditions align with your strategy. This brings us to Timing.

Your ability to be cautious without being fearful will determine your Timing. You are responsible for weighing your Spirit against your Impact and balancing them out with reason. When your Timing is in alignment with your environment, you can resist impulsive actions from the gut and make sure you don't rush into anything too quickly.

How carefully have you studied your environment? You can never do too much due diligence. What's changing around you? Does it make sense to take action now, or should you spend more time understanding why the environment is this way and how it might change in the future? Will your next action be a case of one step forward, two steps back? Also, consider the difference between patience vs procrastination. While you want to be cautious, you don't want to miss an opportunity. You can know the difference between the two by considering how your level of precaution looks from the perspective of your cabinet members.

Use the mirror test to evaluate how you feel in your gut, heart, and mind. Make sure these three factors are in alignment and not competing with each other to dictate your next action. If you find yourself jumping into a plan of action when you feel doubt deep inside, or saying, "Let's go! What's the big deal?" without first analyzing your environment, you are taking steps before rationalizing. This is the writing on the wall that says, "There is a misalignment!"

For example, if you have a gut feeling about what needs to be done and perform adequate due diligence to decide how to accomplish your goal, you might discover another more meaningful goal to pursue instead. However, if there's no fire in your heart, or if your goal won't impact those around you in a healthy way, don't do it. You're not in alignment with your environment and immediate action won't bring about long term success.

If you're passionate, but your gut is holding you back, listen to your instinct. When your due diligence suggests you might be heading into a trap, don't listen to your passion. If you really want to go skydiving with a burning passion, but once you get up in the air your body just won't let you jump, don't force yourself. You are not fully in alignment with your environment and your next action might be regrettable.

If you consider every option and chase every lead, but you lack instinct or passion, all your work might be a waste of time because it doesn't fulfill your true Spirit. A higher quality of life and an enriched experience of your present moment are possible. Even if the progress you're making will have a positive impact on your environment, feeling dispassionate about your work prevents you from aligning with the position you are in. If you're misaligned with the environment, your approach to achieving your goals is not efficient.

You want to know that it's "All Systems Go" before taking action. Assess your head, heart, and gut, and then run your plan of action by the people on your panel. If they concur that you're on track, in full alignment, and don't have blind spots in your reasoning, passion, or impact, go for it! You've likely devised an incredibly efficient way to get closer to your desired outcome.

When you aren't in alignment with one or more of these factors, including your environment, you are on an inefficient path. This will lead to missteps and drive you away from your goal with astonishing speed, then you'll have to retrace your steps all the way back to the Track of Humility and start over again from the beginning. Remember, failing does not necessarily mean you acted in misalignment with these factors, especially if you learn from your failure. Sometimes, failure can be the most productive step in reaching your goal. So learn to become comfortable with failure, and fail well. Every experience is a success. You just need to understand that you successfully figured out how not to do something.

What Happens When You're Misaligned

You will find that your actions and values become misaligned when you experience a void between yourself and the universe. It's uncomfortable to feel misaligned. It is a state in which your ambitions and actions don't line up with reality. To fill the void, we are tempted to gravitate toward the Dark, Negative Attitude and distort our perceptions to create false alignment, first through the Grandiose Mindset and eventually through the Despair Mindset.

For example, if you really want a promotion, but there is no opening for the new job you are interested in, your environment and timing are not lined up with your desire to get promoted. You might fall into a Grandiose Mindset and start to think you're too good for a job that doesn't recognize your talents. This may lead you into conflict with management expecting them to create the opening for you. Soon you might fall into a Despair Mindset and start to think you'll never get a promotion no matter how hard you try.

Neither of these mindsets are productive in helping you get you to your goal of achieving that promotion. They take you off the Track of Humility onto an unproductive emotional track, and they compromise your Efficiency. Ultimately, these mindsets emerge when we make rapid decisions, acting to fill the void as fast as possible at the expense of finding an effective solution. This moves you in the wrong direction.

We all have fallen into the trap of rushing through our decisions because we want to bring immediate closure to a situation. It makes us anxious and uneasy to operate in the middle ground between the beginning and end of an emotional situation, so we rush for closure. We want a conclusion so we can ease our discomfort and move away from the middle ground as fast as possible. But pushing for premature closure often puts us on the wrong road entirely.

Jumping to conclusions is a trap. We think it will help us avoid anxiety and uncertainty, but allowing our emotional impulses to run wild leads us to use quick fixes instead of Efficient and well-planned strategies.

What To Do When You're Misaligned

Sometimes the environment is in alignment your goals, but and sometimes it isn't, and this creates uncertainty and anxiety. When this happens, trying to push forward is inefficient. Instead, become aware of your uncertainty and embrace it. Understand that sometimes the answer is "no answers yet," and we need to be okay with not knowing how everything will turn out.

Recognize that there is a natural process to align with your environment and reach closure. Once you can embrace your feelings of uncertainty, use your Imagination and Values to outline a plan to achieve your goals. Don't take shortcuts. As you follow your plan, stay patient, understanding, and aware. Adjust your path if necessary and remind yourself that you will bring your vision to life if you are persistent and calculated. Make every second count toward the pursuit of your goal but avoid jumping to conclusions too quickly. It can be stressful to stay on the Track of Humility for ages without noticing much progress toward your goal, especially when there's a tantalizing shortcut you're dying to try out, tapping away like a distracting woodpecker in the back of your mind.

To resist wasting time with inefficient shortcuts, you must be able to withstand emotional pressure. It's uncomfortable to be misaligned with your goals, but succumbing to that pressure and acting on emotional impulse—or giving in to your Dark, Negative emotions—will restrict how far you go in life.

When you're faced with these inner challenges, you can build emotional muscles. View every challenge as an opportunity to become more comfortable with the unknown. Develop the ability to endure more pressure by practicing humility. Take responsibility for your position and make the changes necessary within yourself to align your inner Spirit, Impact, and Timing with your goals and Environment.

Sometimes, there is a power outside our control that prevents us from attaining our goals. Respect these uncontrollable environmental forces. For example, if you ask someone out on a date and they reject you, it probably won't do you much good to start a debate about why the two of you should go out. The other person's disinterest is out of your control and you don't have the power to change their mind. It's uncomfortable, but you must accept that misalignment of your goal and your environment with humility. You're not the center of the universe and things won't always go your way. This discomfort builds strength. Accept it with humility and it will help you become the person you want to be.

Step 1 of Efficiency is the most critical step. If you can align your three lenses of Spirit, Impact, and Timing with your Environment, you're on your way to tuning the three lenses of Imagination, Values, and Efficiency into a greater vision of the future too. Your 20/20 foresight is coming into focus!

2. Learn to Expand Opportunities with Humility

Humility and Efficiency are deeply linked. When we're humble about our capacity for learning, we can become more efficient learners. When we become more efficient learners, we can discern healthy ways to stay on track.

Being humble about your learning abilities means recognizing where you struggle and where you excel. Confusing weaknesses for strengths leads to a distorted self image, propelling you off the Track of Humility and into the pitfalls. At the same time, if you are confident in your ability to learn, you can find an efficient way to acquire any information you need. In other words, be a humble learner so you can accurately assess how you learn best and which techniques work for you.

Understanding your learning curve creates genuine confidence because it gives you a firm understanding of how long it will take to absorb any new information. Perhaps math is a breeze for you, so watching a few video lessons and scratching down a handful of practice problems is enough to lock in a novel numerical concept. You'll know what methods might aid your under-standing of a certain math problem, meaning you can budget your time effi-ciently and you won't get stuck anywhere. You shouldn't rest on your laurels, though. Past success doesn't guarantee future success, so every problem should be approached with an open mindset and due diligence just in case it's more complicated than you expected.

On the other hand, if compiling a budget report feels like pulling teeth to you, be confident in that shortcoming. Be honest with yourself about the fact that it takes you twice as long to do these types of tasks. You might even want to get a fact check from a qualified peer to make sure your work is error free. If you want to overcome this shortcoming and become an expert on budget sheets, you can efficiently make a plan to achieve a better understanding.

The disciplined approach to learning humility starts with knowing yourself. Ask yourself how you learn, what tools help you, what techniques hinder you, and how you operate when faced with different material to comprehend. Understanding where you have inefficient learning habits will help you adjust your approach. In the case of compiling a budget report you might jump to conclusions and make a purchase based on a misunderstanding of your budget. If so, you're not being Efficient in your actions. You'll then have to reverse the purchase or recoup your losses, consult the budget sheet again, then go out and make a more informed decision.

This is another example of slowing down in the short run to save time in the long run. One way to compensate for your learning inefficiencies is to ask your panel to help you stay humble. Tell them you're seeking their expertise because you know they have insight to help you become a better learner.

Approaching your learning with humility will increase your self-confidence and add to your emotional resilience, allowing you take on more pressure the next time you go toe-to-toe with a budget sheet that looks like it's written in ancient hieroglyphics.

Learning from a place of arrogance is a different story entirely. The type of people who refuse to admit their shortcomings, fail to ask for help, and rest on their laurels often give up when they hit a roadblock. They forfeit the opportunity to grow from a challenge or learn something new. Instead, they generally start to transfer blame and make excuses for their lack of comprehension. They might think they are smart enough to understand a new concept, but an unconscious road block could be preventing them from truly grasping it. This demonstrates a lack of humility, Efficiency, and dedication to learning. This mentality feeds right into the traps that fall on either side of the Track of Humility.

3. Instinct Alone Will Lead to Ruin

As discussed in Step 1, Instinct is your gut feeling, and it shouldn't be left unchecked or you'll run into serious problems. When you encounter new challenges, it's easy to respond with the first action that pops into your head. We often do what feels right rather than thinking critically. This gut reaction leads to jumping to conclusions, which is terribly inefficient. Even though trusting your gut requires less time and energy than thinking deeply, it will often leave you in the wrong place, and that can send shockwaves through your entire being. Your confidence in your instincts will erode. As a result, you might stop listening to your gut feelings entirely, discounting them as wrong. This isn't the best way forward. In reality, we should listen to our instincts, just not exclusively.

Additionally, if our instinctual choices lead to undesirable outcomes, we might outsource the blame and pat ourselves on the back for having the right instinct regardless. Then we'll continue down the wrong track towards Entitlement and Charlatanism.

Relying on instinct alone can lead to a variety of problems and ultimately it can erode your reputation and credibility. Once a cucumber becomes a pickle it will never be a cucumber again. Don't pickle your reputation.

Case 1

Imagine you are chatting with a loved one, a coworker, or someone else you've spent considerable time with. They begin to say something and you quickly interrupt, filling in the blanks and discounting what they're going to say. Your instinct is saying you already know where the conversation is going, so you decide it would be more efficient to just say it yourself. Which is wrong. You've changed the direction of the conversation, but you haven't actually heard your companion. Instead, you've taken an action that erodes respect in the relationship. You then begin to earn a bad reputation because you seem to be rushing to get the conversation "over with."

This can be avoided very easily by slowing down your response to give yourself time to consider the other person and what they have to say. If someone comes to you for help, help them by making it about them and not you.

Case 2

You're on your way to meet someone for dinner at a new restaurant. You've never seen it before, but you have a vague idea of where it is. You checked a map to confirm its address then you hopped in the car and started driving without typing the address into a navigator. Your instinct tells you it will be easy to find. But then, where's the restaurant? You spend 20 minutes searching before realizing you took a wrong turn, then you finally pull over and use a navigator to look up the restaurant. You see your mistake but now you're 40 minutes late.

Even if your gut tells you to press forward, overconfidence can send you down the wrong path. Use reasoning and humility to keep your gut in check.

Case 3

A new member was just added to your team at work, and something about him is off. Is it his hair? No, maybe it's the way he talks, it's so lurid. Or maybe it's his pants… Whatever instinctual prejudgment you're making of this person could be entirely wrong. In fact, after a few weeks of working together a time comes when you discover your misjudgment. Up to that point, your relationship with this person has been horribly inefficient because you treated him like someone he was not. And the longer you try to cram all of the new data you receive about this person into your instinctual idea of who he really is, the longer it will take to have a quality working relationship.

You might get the impression that your coworker is the type of person who will act a certain way based on your gut reaction, but operating on your preconceived notions can lead to inefficient misalignments and damaged relationships.

It's okay to use your instinct, but counterbalance it. Ask yourself how your heart and mind disagree with your gut. Your instinctual decision in a certain situation might be something your heart doesn't like. You can use your head to slow yourself down, weigh your heart against the gut, evaluate the pros and cons, and find a way to take the next best step forward.

Hint: The next best step is the one that aligns your heart and gut together! Jumping to conclusions is wrong when it pits your gut and heart against each other.

4. Understanding Shifts in Your Environment and Serving Your Relationships

People are dynamic creatures. We are not static, predictable beings. Treating people as unchanging will hurt your relationships, while adapting to changes efficiently will maintain your relationships.

The discipline of studying and understanding the everchanging qualities of the people we interact with will makes others feel seen and heard deeply. In a simple example, if you and your boyfriend enjoy going out for tea and one day your boyfriend becomes more of a coffee guy, would you keep buying him tea for Christmas? He's still the same person, but his interests have changed. Understanding this shift will allow for better harmony in the relationship. With this understanding, you might get him a French press for Christmas—instead of another tin of oolong he's less inclined to use—so he'll cherish your gift instead of feeling like you don't understand him.

If your boyfriend is usually very level-headed, but begins to respond to high-pressure situations with panic instead of calm, his personality might be changing. He might not be as patient as he used to be, so you may encourage him to hone his patience and he might be able to shift back to his calm, peaceful self. However, bringing up highly-stressful topics without regard to the new way stress affects him will probably damage the relationship. Further, if your boyfriend cannot find a way to become peaceful again, understanding this shift in his personality might encourage you to get out of the relationship so you don't hurt each other with impatient arguments.

There are two types of changes you'll notice in others. While people can change their interests frequently, they don't shift their personality nearly as often. It's critical to evaluate whether a shift in someone else's behavior reflects a personality change or an interest change. In most cases you will discover it's an interest change. So how can you tell the difference?

The key to identifying a personality shift is to pay attention to someone's attitude when they're doing something they don't enjoy. It's easy to temper your expressions when you aren't under pressure. However, if you're not enjoying something, it takes a lot of effort to hide your dismay. True personalities come out under stress, greed, or the influence of drugs and alcohol, so monitor people's reactions to these conditions.

To gauge the shifts in someone's interests, check in and listen to them without judgment. When you stay open, observant, and genuinely interested in a relationship with someone you will naturally notice countless movements of their interests. Operating on the pretense that a person's interests are static will influence us to jump to conclusions. We might assume we have someone figured out instead of listening to the changes in their lives. This is one way our relationships can become misaligned. We start to distort our perceptions of people to get them to conform to our impressions, which damages relationships. To be efficient in maintaining healthy relationships, we must be disciplined against our own selfish desires to assume.

5. Respect the Credentials of Your Panel to Bring Initiatives to Life

Abraham Lincoln was an Efficient president because he surrounded himself with the right people for the right jobs. He didn't necessarily get along with his cabinet members, but he respected their credentials to no end. He had a vision and knew it was necessary to sacrifice personal and political disputes to bring his initiatives to life. And he did.

Respecting the credentials of your panel means understanding each member. It means understanding how much weight to give their insight on different areas. It means admitting when you need help and utilizing the right people to cover your blindspots. It would be an inefficient use of the people in your corner if you failed to understand their strengths and weaknesses and asked them to help with problems they might not be excellent at solving. That would be like a military chief suddenly assigning his sword-fighters to pick up longbows. Or a CEO asking her finance people to switch over to his sales department. This type of inefficiency can lead to even more blindspots.

The key here is to find people with credentials to help you instead of seeking assistance from someone who doesn't really know what they're talking about. Unbeknownst to you, the wrong advisor might take you off track and into the pitfalls. They could feed into your blindspots instead of illuminating them. They may tell you what you want to hear instead of their true observations.

Respecting the credentials of your panel also means not asking the same questions to every cabinet member. If you get too much input from everyone, you'll be in a too-many-cooks situation. Lincoln guarded against this by leaving his door open to only his closest circle and reserving his questions for the appropriate advisors. It would be terribly inefficient to consider the advice of the Secretary of Agriculture on equal ground as a tip from the Secretary of Defense when you have a question about the possibility of a nuclear war. To bring your initiatives to life, keep most of your questions within your panel and direct each specific inquiry to the person with the most suitable credentials on the subject of concern.

6. Recall the Two Motivators: Fear of Loss and Hope of Gain

The sixth step for greater Efficiency is to remember that we are motivated by Fear of Loss and Hope for Gain. Our most efficient energy comes when we are powered by the balance of these two. When we can find this balance on the Track of Humility we will feel an invisible tension within, pushing us to do what we're set out to do. This means not focusing exclusively on hope or on loss, as these will lead to the Pitfalls. Finding humility in the middle will lead us on the most direct path toward our goals. Intense hope and fear are only detours.

Imagine holding two quarter-sized magnets about one inch apart. You can feel the invisible energy. Hope is your desire for change, and fear is your desire to hold onto what you have. Between these two posts you can generate the energy to move forward.

Staying in the middle relates back to the First Checkpoint, setting realistic expectations for yourself. If you're overly hopeful or fearful, you will experience Grandiosity and veer off the Track of Humility. When you're too hopeful of a positive outcome you are setting your expectations too high. You'll become Grandiose instead of putting in the time and effort necessary to achieve success. Conversely, being too fearful of a negative outcome will also lead to Grandiosity. Fear of failure might prevent you from even attempting to achieve your goals, telling yourself instead that you're too good to even try. Or you might fear that something will go wrong and act right away to reduce uncertainty anxiety instead of stopping to perform due diligence.

Take the example of looking to buy a new car. It's not good to be too hopeful about the purchase. If you dance onto the lot in a fit of joy, you might buy the first good-looking car you see without taking time to evaluate it accurately. The next thing you know you're in a vehicle that isn't right for you. Now you're disappointed and start thinking about trading it for a better car, which costs more time and money. Being too hopeful is not efficient. In this example, it leads to remorse.

Fear is also an idealized vision for the future. In this case, you might be motivated by your desire to avoid making a bad decision. You anticipate that if you hurry up and pick something, you'll extinguish your fears. *If I just buy this car today, those scary feelings will go away.* Ironically, you'll bring your fear to life because you haven't taken the proper steps to arrive at your desired outcome. Once again, you'll waste time and energy trading in your less-than-desirable car for another. Again, you'll find yourself dealing with a remorseful outcome.

Operating systematically in between hope and fear will allow you to slow down and make the right evaluations to inform your next step. It will certainly take longer to run a careful analysis of your position instead of just going with what feels right, but the end result will bring you closer to your goal instead of farther from it. For this reason, staying in the power zone is what propels you to your goals.

Operating with Efficiency

To operate with efficiency we must align our Spirit, Impact, and Timing, with our Environment. To bring ourselves into alignment with an environment we often cannot control, we need to follow the remaining five steps.

By cultivating healthy learning habits we can efficiently acquire more information and remain humble about our position in our environment as we seek to align ourselves with it. By weighing our gut instinct against our heart and mind, we can slow down and steer clear of decisions that will take us out of alignment. Next, we can observe that the people in our environment are changing as much as we are. Shifting our own actions to better relate to others will improve the quality of our relationships. These quality relationships will lead to us having more people in our corner who support us as we head towards our goals. Respecting the credentials of these people will help us take the next best step to align ourselves with our environment and achieve our goals. Finally, finding a balance between Hope for Gain and Fear of Loss will prevent us from acting impulsively to quell negative emotions, which would push our Spirit, Impact, and Timing out of alignment.

These steps are all interconnected, and they come down to one basic principle: to be efficient, you have to slow down to speed up. Take your time. Be patient. Do your due diligence. Resist emotional impulses. Don't jump to conclusions. When you take the time to evaluate your position and your alignment, you can stay on the Track of Humility and take the best step instead of the quickest step. Master this and you'll be in alignment with your environment.

Efficiency is the third of the three Elements for deepening greater foresight. In the final chapter I'll demonstrate how to utilize all the skills we've discussed to achieve a greater vision of the future…

Chapter 9
A Greater Vision of the Future

When you think of Foresight, what imagery comes to mind? Is it a gaze into a crystal ball, foretelling a future fate? A sort of "spidey-sense," or a chill down your spine before some terrible event? Or is it a feeling deep down that you know what's next?

None of these sensations describe the reality of Foresight. These things might be fun to imagine, but they're not realistic examples of seeing into the future. In fact, there are zero reliable ways of predicting what will happen next. This is because the most meaningful, influential events are also the most unpredictable. Who could have guessed the Titanic would sink or the Hindenburg would explode? Can any traders on Wall Street truly guarantee they will make any money? Could Buddy Holly have known his pilot was untrained to fly in low-visibility conditions, dooming their voyage from the start? Researchers have been unable to uncover any solid evidence of people who possess the psychic ability to foresee future events. Developing Foresight is not about learning how to predict the future.

Foresight is a skill that combines confidence, self-awareness, and emotional stability. It is the ability to evaluate your current position and decide your next best step. It's a deep sense that you can navigate the uncharted path ahead, resistant to forces that might try to lead you astray. Developing Foresight is the accumulation of everything in this book, and it is the best way to achieve a greater future for yourself.

Confidence is a key component for Foresight. Operating without confidence makes us vulnerable to loss aversion, ego-protection, following the crowd, and gravitating toward unrealistic expectations. It takes confidence to admit you don't have all the answers and shouldn't make an irreversible decision before you've gathered more information. And once you've made your decision, it takes confidence to know that you've done your thorough research and have a strong reason for placing your bet, changing jobs, or breaking up with your significant other. With confidence, you can perform due diligence, evaluate your situation, and take the next step without letting insecurity pull you off the Track of Humility.

Foresight also requires self-awareness because ignoring your strengths and weaknesses can result in misalignments that don't help you get closer to your goal. Overestimating your skills or underestimating your weaknesses can send you careening for the pitfalls as you develop a Grandiose Mindset. If your self-image doesn't align with the actual person you see in the mirror, you will be more inclined to operate with the Dark, Negative Attitude, filling your imagination with unhealthy distortions. From there it is a slippery slope toward the Charlatan and Discreditable Mindsets as your distortions refute even the most watertight contrary evidence. Any indication you aren't making the right decision will be swallowed up by the void.

To use Foresight, stay in the invisible, yet powerful, neutral zone between fear of loss and hope for gain. We all have strong emotions that can pull us off the Track of Humility and put us on another emotional track. When we're having a bad day because the rain is pouring, our car battery is dead, and we're stuck in the cold, it can seem like nothing ever goes our way. When we're deeply in love with someone who fills our days with joy, it can seem like nothing could ever go wrong. Like confidence, emotional stability prevents us from being impulsive with our decision making and allows us to widen our scope. And like self-awareness, emotional stability helps us see a less-distorted view of ourselves and our environment so we can act in alignment with what's really happening, not what we hope or fear might happen. We all experience intense emotional states at times, but getting back to neutral before a major decision is a fundamental piece of acting with Foresight.

Emotional stability, confidence, and self-awareness are the building blocks of Foresight. When we understand ourselves, see our current situation without distortion, and imagine an informed path to our goal, we are acting with Foresight. This ability allows us to see what's likely ahead on our path so we can consistently take productive actions that propel us toward our greater vision of the future.

Staying on Track

Humility and Foresight go hand in hand. When you're on the Track of Humility, you maximize your ability to foresee what might lie ahead on the path to your goal. However, there are five powerful forces that will try to pull you off track. This book has covered all five in depth, so with your understanding of previous chapters you should be able to connect these influences to Foresight. To make this connection clearer, I'll use a visual example from a well-known adage: Measure twice, cut one.

If you're a carpenter who is trying to cut a two-by-eight plank of wood into two identical two-by-fours, you need to ensure that your measurement of the midpoint is accurate before you cut, or you'll have two uneven and useless pieces of wood. Once you've cut the board, that's it. There's no undo button. Instead of taking a step towards completing your deck repairs before sundown, you'll be further from your goal and in need of shelling out more time, money, and effort to drive to Home Depot for another piece of wood.

There are five ways you can make the wrong measurement and therefore the wrong next cut. You'll recognize them as Failing the Three Checkpoints, Experiencing Early Success, Filling the Void, Ignoring Blindspots, and Falling onto Emotional Tracks.

1. Three Checkpoints

Failing to pass through any of the three Checkpoints is the first way to end up in one of the pitfalls. To make it through the first checkpoint, we need to know where we are going. If you don't know exactly how you're going to repair the deck, how can you know how much wood to cut to finish the job? A misevaluation of his position is what led pilot Roger Peterson to take off unprepared and crash his plane, killing everyone on board.

The second checkpoint is about taking responsibility. If you double-check your measurement and see that it's off, don't blame the tape measure. Blame yourself for making a mistake and look at what you can do to fix the problem. The managers of the Winter Dance Party tour avoided responsibility for the wellbeing of the musicians and created a dangerous schedule. When the band members suffered in the cold, the managers could have stepped up and said, "Yeah, a 400-mile trek through the snow isn't a good idea. Our mistake. Let's reschedule so no one gets burnt out." But they didn't. They didn't think it was their fault that the musicians were stressed out, so after the plane crash, they asked the surviving band members to keep playing in the same torturous conditions.

Checkpoint three is about being honest with yourself. Buddy Holly wasn't acting with Foresight when he decided to stay on the road despite signs that the tour was in danger. He wasn't honest with himself about his pain or the pain of those around him. Instead of reassessing the health of his peers and quitting the tour, he made a life-ending decision to charter a plane. When cutting a plank of wood, be realistic about your ability to make the cut. If you think you have it under control, but your measurements are slightly off, you could cut your hand in the process or build something unsafe.

Falling into traps at any of the Three Checkpoints means you aren't measuring twice before you cut. Instead of operating with Foresight, you're straying from your goal. To remain on the Track of Humility and act with Foresight, respect the Three Checkpoints.

2. Danger of Success

Success can also take us off the Track of Humility and ruin our Foresight. When we experience early success, we'll be tempted to inflate our ego, double down if proven wrong, and hold tight to our process instead of evaluating ourselves and thinking honestly about whether we got lucky. If you measure twice before cutting and see that your measurements were spot-on, don't rest on your laurels. This initial success can create a false sense of confidence that pulls you off the Track of Humility. Next time you go to make a cut, you might only measure once to save time. Why measure twice when you were precise as a laser beam last time? Well, your measurements can still be wrong, so don't take previous successes as an excuse for future corner-cutting. Measure twice in every situation regardless of past experiences so you don't make the wrong cut next time. If you have Foresight, you'll be aware that something could go wrong at any point and prepare by measuring twice no matter what. This way, you'll ensure perfect cuts.

3. Filling the Void

Filling the Void with distortions is the third danger that can pull you off the Track of Humility because it prevents you from making realistic measurements before you cut. It's impossible to operate with Foresight and make the next best step when the ground beneath you is warped. Imagine the plank you're working with has a massive knot in the center, or a warp that curves to one side. Recognizing the reality that you're dealing with a tricky piece of wood might compel you to go to the lumberyard for a replacement. But if you distort the wood by clamping it into a straighter alignment before you measure, you'll be left with a warped cut when you unclamp. Further, if you pretend that the knot in the middle isn't a big deal because you'd rather risk cutting into it than go back to the store, you could be in for a horrible disaster. Cutting straight into a dense, splintery knot cut could shatter the wood, sending shrapnel into your eye, ruining your vision and your project. Don't fill the void by pretending that problems aren't there. Don't try to use illusions to bend the world to your will. Sometimes we will have misalignments, but if we fail to understand them, we won't take accurate measurements and therefore we will lose our Foresight.

4. Blindspots

Blindspots are the fourth factor that can pull us off the Track of Humility and ruin our Foresight. In order to take the next best step, we need to be honest with ourselves, which means being confident in the fact that we don't know everything. President Lincoln operated with humility and asked his rivals for advice so he could maximize his Foresight as a leader. Historians largely attribute his immense success to his ability to compensate for his blindspots through the expertise of his closest advisors.

If you've never swung a hammer or drilled a nail in your life, how can you expect to repair your deck all by yourself? This woodworking project is riddled with blindspots! You might measure twice, but are your blueprints accurate? Is the wood treated to withstand outdoor weather conditions? Do you have the right tools for the job? Simply measuring the length of the wood twice is not enough to ensure a perfect cut and a repaired deck. If you don't know exactly what you're doing, don't make the cut until you consult a close advisor who has substantial woodworking skills to cover those blindspots. Ignoring your blindspots is the opposite of operating with Foresight.

5. Emotional Tracks

Emotional stability is paramount to developing Foresight, so it's no surprise that being pulled onto negative or positive Emotional Tracks can inhibit our ability to achieve our goals. If we spend too much time daydreaming about the perfectly repaired deck with our family around barbequing and having drinks in the summer, we might be so excited we lose focus and cut without measuring. The resulting miscut will halt our progress and delay the party. Focusing on your vision of the party is not productive because you are skipping a few steps. Before you can party, you must build a solid foundation (the deck) to celebrate upon. Foresight means seeing the importance of an accurate cut and repair job before planning the barbeque.

On the other hand, if you find woodworking to be an absolute drag, the

Emotional Track of boredom might take hold. In a bored mindset you might rush to get the project over with as soon as possible. Failing to measure twice in this situation is not a step in the right direction, rather it makes the project take even longer if we botch the cut. Nervousness about the accuracy of the cut can also lead to an error. Arrogance that we can eyeball anything can lead to a miscut as well. Fear that we won't finish the deck by the time guests arrive for the party is another emotional track that can lead to a screwup. Emotional Tracks inhibit Foresight and prevent us from taking the next best step.

When you measure twice and cut once, you're analyzing everything in your ever-changing environment to ensure you make the next best step towards a desired outcome. It requires awareness of these five influences so you can navigate around them with precision and care. Healthy confidence, self-awareness, and emotional neutrality can keep these influences in check as we operate on the Track of Humility and develop Foresight. Further, we can boil down confidence, self-awareness, and emotional stability to one overarching value: Independence.

Understanding Independence

Adopting an independent mindset is crucial for cultivating confidence, self-awareness, and emotional stability. However, being independent doesn't mean tuning out everyone else. Strategically relying on others doesn't make you any less of an independent person. There is a key difference between asking for help and a lack of independence.

Complete dependence is incredibly unhealthy. It means you cannot function on your own. A dependent person bases their successes and failures on others instead of evaluating their own personal role in the outcomes. When a dependent person succeeds, they tell themself it happened because the stars magically aligned, not because of their efforts. Or they might fall into the Entitlement mindset, clinging to the success to support their Grandiose self-image and ignoring the actions that led to success in the first place. When a dependent person experiences a failure, they believe it has nothing to do with their actions. They imagine failure is always someone else's fault because a dependent person would rather preserve their ego than face reality. For a dependent person, saving face is an art form.

Contrarily, strategically relying on others means having the confidence to ask for an expert's help to evaluate your measurement before you cut. True independence doesn't mean we are self-sufficient or bulletproof. We all need advisors. An independent individual strategically relies on the people in their corner to help them measure their next move, especially when they need expertise to cover their blindspots. If an expert in your corner makes a mistake that leads to a bad cut, stay on the Track of Humility by taking responsibility for the mistake yourself because you asked for the expert's help in the first place. The independent person admits they had a blindspot, put their faith in the wrong person, and ended up with an undesirable outcome. This mindset hones Foresight. The Independent person learns they should do more research and potentially make a different choice the next time they face a similar obstacle. Instead of blaming the expert for causing the error, the independent person accepts responsibility 110% of the time. To master Foresight, recognize that the buck stops with you every time.

True Independence is the greatest gift of all. It allows you to steer clear of Grandiosity, Entitlement, Despair, and all the other pitfalls. It allows for more accurate appraisals of your position so you can set healthy expectations, stay on the neutral track, and gradually propel yourself to your goal.

We cannot bring ourselves to independence through sheer will alone. We must perform a full inventory check, becoming aware of our strengths and shortcomings. We must make daily reflections in the mirror to know exactly where we are, who we are, and where we want to go.

Becoming aware of our strengths means making sure we have a crystal clear view of our current position as it relates to our life. Becoming aware of shortcomings means critically evaluating ourselves without judgement. We must accept our insecurities so we can bring them to the table openly, without feeling shame or inadequacy. Once we take on responsibility and acknowledge our strengths and weaknesses, we can further understand how to align our actions with our greater vision for the future.

This is a process that requires healthy, truthful feedback from the people in our corner (whether we want to hear it or not). When we accept this feedback, we must resist fighting it with strong emotions! Instead, work to accept and take in the criticism without reacting to it.

Gathering criticism doesn't mean "fixing" ourselves, because people are not broken. All the problems that arise from a lack of Foresight are based in unawareness, not inadequacy. We fall into the traps because we are unaware of our strengths and weaknesses, not because we are flawed. We must see ourselves without distortion to gain a true picture of our position, or else we'll be knocked off the Track of Humility by the Checkpoints, Early Success, Misalignments, Blindspots, or Emotional Tracks.

To reach this awareness, we need emotional strength. It might not be easy to see past our distortions, which is why we need confidence to become more independent. We gain confidence by slowing our reactions and responses to events so that we can take educated courses of action, rather than impulsive ones. By practicing daily reflections in the mirror and challenging ourselves to respond to feedback in a healthy way, we will become emotionally stronger, more Independent, and less likely to be pulled off the Track of Humility. In this way, Independence is a natural byproduct of confidence, self-awareness, and emotional strength. It is the most valuable characteristic to developing Foresight.

Mastering the Three Elements

When we achieve Independence we will be able to effectively master and utilize the Three Elements so we can further expand our Foresight.

First, Imagination is all about considering every possible option, outcome, and opportunity before taking action. An Independent person is able to more effectively practice the Element of Imagination because they will not be swayed by their judgements into ruling out certain next steps prematurely. By using Imagination to consider a wider range of possibilities, an Independent person develops greater Foresight.

The Second Element, Values, revolves around respect for yourself and others. When a person has true Independence, they will be able to see their position for what it really is, not what they want it to be. Therefore, they can do the right things, in the right ways, for the right reasons, instead of acting based on selfish distortions. In this way, an Independent person is more resistant to the irrational influences that could pull them off the Track of Humility, while becoming attracted to healthy next steps that respect all parties. As we aim to take the actions that are most in line with our Values, we can hone our Foresight to focus on what's best, not what's most convenient.

Efficiency is the Third Element of deep foresight and it is based on operating in the neutral zone. Independence allows us to stay emotionally neutral more often because when we are more independent we will be less obsessed with what others might think of us. This gets us out of an ego-protection mindset. Without focusing on Fear of Loss or Hope for Gain, an Independent person can see further ahead down the Track of Humility and take the proper steps to ensure they stay on the straight and narrow. The emotional tracks and mindset pitfalls won't pull an Independent person out of alignment as easily as they might with a dependent person. Therefore Independence can allow us to act with Efficiency so we can maintain Foresight as often as possible.

None of this works until we can each accept that we are responsible for all that we do. Grasping this understanding helps us stay Independent and keeps us on the Track of Humility.

Seeing With Foresight

Foresight is not the ability to predict the future, it is the emotional capacity to navigate the future without the anxiety, depression, or distortions that might knock us off course.

To develop Foresight, act with the Three Elements. To master the Elements, operate with Independence. To learn Independence, practice confidence, self-awareness, and emotional stability with daily reflections in the mirror and an openness to critical feedback.

Developing Foresight is a lifelong practice, but it's entirely achievable by anybody with the determination to realize a better life. In this book, you have all the tools you need to become aware of the Track of Humility and stay out of the pitfalls. Plus, if you ever lose sight, you can always flip open *Foresight is 20/20* to the chapter you need most for a refresher. Consider this book a secret weapon in your corner to help you when you aren't sure which step is the next best step. With enough practice, you'll be able to stay on the Track of Humility in even the most trying of situations. You'll be able to achieve your greater vision of the future instead of spending your life savings on a motorcycle that isn't what you thought it was.

I know you can do it. You know you can do it. Close this book and look in the mirror. Choose this very second to begin your new journey.

Notes

Introduction

"There are just ten John Britten V1000s in existence" - Lenatsch, N. (2016, April 14). Britten V1000: On The Gas Racing the Britten proves just how ahead of its time the V1000 was. Retrieved November 13, 2020, from https://www.cycleworld.com/john-britten-v1000-racebike-motorcycle-riding-and-racing-experience/

"a wide front fairing seated above an extra narrow engine assembly, like a torpedo atop a knife blade" - Terlick, P. (2017, February 25). The home-made bike that conquered the world; the Britten V1000. Retrieved November 13, 2020, from https://www.bikeshedtimes.com/the-home-made-bike-that-conquered-the-world-the-britten-v1000/

"Britten famously shaped his bikes on a chicken wire frame covered in clay" - Winn, N. (2015). Why The Britten V1000 Is The Most Incredible Built-Not-Bought Bike Ever Made. Retrieved November 13, 2020, from https://www.carthrottle.com/post/why-the-britten-v1000-is-the-most-incredible-built-not-bought-bike-ever-made/

"The first person to notice it was Al Lambert" - The Cole Rodriguez story, including the comments from Al Lambert and Mary Warsaw, have been fictionalized for the purposes of illustrating the grandiose mindset.

"And it only makes up about 1% of our field of vision" - Johnson, Jeff, and Kate Finn. *Designing User Interfaces for an Aging Population: towards Universal Design.* Amsterdam: Morgan Kaufmann, 2017.

"an area known as the fovea centralis" - Yamada, E. (1969). Some Structural Features of the Fovea Centralis in the Human Retina. Archives of Opthamology, 82(2), 151-159. doi:10.1001/archopht.1969.00990020153002

"This phenomenon of selective attention has since been nicknamed The Invisible Gorilla" - Chabris, C., & Simons, D. (2010). The Invisible Gorilla: How Our Intuitions Deceive Us. New York, NY: Random House.

"A lot of what we see and conclude about the world is authored by our brains" - Resnick, Brian. 2019. "An Expert on Human Blind Spots Gives Advice on How to Think." Vox. January 31, 2019. https://www.vox.com/science-and-health/2019/1/31/18200497/dunning-kruger-effect-explained-trump.

"it's a universal human bias" - Dunning, David. 2011. "The Dunning–Kruger Effect." Advances in Experimental Social Psychology 44: 247–96. https://doi.org/10.1016/b978-0-12-385522-0.00005-6.

"their 1999 paper titled *Unskilled and Unaware of It*" - Kruger, Justin, and David Dunning. 1999. "Unskilled and Unaware of It: How Difficulties in Recognizing One's Own Incompetence Lead to Inflated Self-Assessments." Journal of Personality and Social Psychology 77 (6): 1121–34. https://doi.org/10.1037/0022-3514.77.6.1121.

"A national survey of Americans revealed that 21% believe they are 'very

likely' or 'fairly likely' to become millionaires within the next ten years"** - Murphy, M. (2017, January 17). The Dunning-Kruger Effect Shows Why Some People Think They're Great Even When Their Work Is Terrible. Retrieved November 13, 2020, from https://www.forbes.com/sites/markmurphy/2017/01/24/the-dunning-kruger-effect-shows-why-some-people-think-theyre-great-even-when-their-work-is-terrible/

"90% of teachers think they are above average" - Cross, K. Patricia. 1977. "Not Can, But will College Teaching Be Improved?" New Directions for Higher Education 1977 (17): 1–15. https://doi.org/10.1002/he.36919771703.

"A survey of several hundred engineers revealed that 32% at one company and 42% at another rated themselves as performing among the top 5% of their peers" - Zenger, Todd. 2017. "The Downside of Full Pay Transparency." Wall Street Journal, August 14, 2017, sec. Business. https://www.wsj.com/articles/the-downside-of-full-pay-transparency-1502676360.

"among medical interns, 80% asserted they understood bladder catheterization well enough to teach it to someone else" - Barnsley, L., Lyon, P., Ralson, S., Hibbert, E., Cunningham, I., Gordon, F., et al. (2004). Clinical skills in junior medical officers: A comparison of self-reported confidence and observed competence. Medical Education, 38, 358–367.

"researchers offered participants a $100 reward if they could accurately guess how they performed on a test" - Ehrlinger, J., Johnson, K., Banner, M., Dunning, D., & Kruger, J. (2008). Why the unskilled are unaware? Further explorations of (lack of) self-insight among the incompetent. Organizational Behavior and Human Decision Processes, 105, 98–121.

"in one study, Dunning asked participants to rate how familiar they were with various terms related to topics like science, politics, and geography" - Critcher, C. R., & Dunning, D. (2009). How chronic self-views influence (and mislead) self-evaluations of performance: Self-views shape bottom-up experiences with the task. Journal of Personality and Social Psychology, 97, 931–945.

"when participants were first asked to calculate 45 + 56 they became more confident they could correctly perform the calculation 45 x 56" - Kruger, J. M., & Dunning, D. (1999). Unskilled and unaware of it: How difficulties in recognizing one's own incompetence lead to inflated self-assessments. Journal of Personality and Social Psychology, 77, 1121–1134.

"most participants were certain they at least knew the basics of how a helicopter works" - Rozenblit, L., & Keil, F. C. (2002). The misunderstood limits of folk science: An illusion of explanatory depth. Cognitive Science, 26, 521–562.

"many people, and women in particular, were unable to correctly position the chain and pedals" - Lawson, Rebecca. 2006. "The Science of Cycology: Failures to Understand How Everyday Objects Work." Memory & Cognition 34 (8): 1667–75. https://doi.org/10.3758/bf03195929.

"The same exact effect has been demonstrated by asking people how well they understand a litany of other common household items" - Rozenblit, Leonid, and Frank Keil. "The misunderstood limits of folk science: An illusion of explanatory depth." Cognitive science 26, no. 5 (2002): 521-562.

"the researchers selected two tasks that were as different as possible: a knowledge assessment and a motor performance test" - West, Richard F., and Keith E. Stanovich. 1997. "The Domain Specificity and Generality of Overconfidence: Individual Differences in Performance Estimation Bias." Psychonomic Bulletin & Review 4 (3): 387–92. https://doi.org/10.3758/bf03210798.

Chapter 1

"Nine months earlier Peterson had failed an instrument checkride..." - Durfee, James R, Chan Gurney, Harmar D Denny, G. Joseph Minetti, and Louis J Hector. "CAB_2-3-1959." Mason City, Iowa: Civil Aeronautics Board, September 23, 1959. Accessed via Wayback Machine online on February 23, 2021; https://web.archive.org/web/20090226025843/https://www.ntsb.gov/Publictn/1959/CAB_2-3-1959.pdf

"The tour began when superstar Buddy Holly decided to join the Winter Dance Party tour with General Artist Corporation." - Norman, Philip. *Buddy: the Definitive Biography of Buddy Holly*. London: Macmillan, 2012.

"The Winter Dance Party tour was scheduled to play in twenty-four Midwestern cities in twenty-four days." - Suddath, Claire. "A Brief History of The Day the Music Died." *Time*, February 3, 2009. Accessed via Wayback Machine online on February 23, 2021; https://web.archive.org/web/20130826140119/http://www.time.com/time/arts/article/0,8599,1876542,00.html

"The tour organizers didn't hire roadies or assistants either." - Huey, Pamela. "Buddy Holly: The Tour from Hell." Star Tribune. Star Tribune, February 3, 2009. https://www.startribune.com/2009-buddy-holly-the-tour-from-hell/38282249/.

"Holly called Valens and Richardson into a private dressing room..." - DiMucci, Dion, and Davin Seay. *The Wanderer: Dion's Story*. New York, NY: Beech Tree Books, 1988.

"Allsup lost out to Valens in a last-minute coin toss." - Press, The Associated. "Tommy Allsup, Guitarist, Dies at 85; a Coin Toss Saved His Life (Published 2017)." The New York Times. The New York Times, January 15, 2017. https://www.nytimes.com/2017/01/13/arts/music/tommy-allsup-guitarist-dies-at-85-a-coin-toss-saved-his-life.html.

"'Well, I hope your plane crashes,' snapped Jennings." - Jennings, Waylon, and Lenny Kaye. *Waylon: an Autobiography*. Chicago, IL: Chicago Review Press, 2012.

"This crash has become known as The Day the Music Died..." - Mikkelson, David. "Did Buddy Holly Die in an Airplane Called 'American Pie'?" Snopes.com, February 3, 2019. https://www.snopes.com/fact-check/american-pie/.

"When we're low on blood sugar, tired, or in a rush, our brain takes shortcuts to accomplish its myriad tasks all at once." - Kahneman, Daniel. "Of 2 Minds: How Fast and Slow Thinking Shape Perception and Choice [Excerpt]." Scientific American. Scientific American, June 15, 2012. https://www.scientificamerican.com/article/kahneman-excerpt-thinking-fast-and-slow/.

"Take the following math problem for example..." - Smith, Andrew R, and Paul D Windschitl. Biased calculations: Numeric anchors influence answers to math equations, February 2011. http://journal.sjdm.org/11/101124/jdm101124.html.

"You might have noticed another phenomenon at play with cupcakes in the breakroom..." - Geier, Andrew B, Paul Rozin, and Gheorghe Doros. "Unit Bias. A New Heuristic That Helps Explain the Effect of Portion Size on Food Intake." Psychological science. U.S. National Library of Medicine, June 2006. https://pubmed.ncbi.nlm.nih.gov/16771803/.

"In one study, participants were asked to rate three pairs of products..." - Lee, Wan-chen Jenny, Mitsuru Shimizu, Kevin M. Kniffin, and Brian Wansink. "You Taste What You See: Do Organic Labels Bias Taste Perceptions?" *Food Quality and Preference* 29, no. 1 (February 9, 2013): 33–39. https://doi.org/10.1016/j.foodqual.2013.01.010.

"One study even allowed participants to sample different wines through a straw while seated in a brain scanner." - Trei, Lisa, and Lisa Trei. "Price Changes Way People Experience Wine, Study Finds." Stanford University, January 16, 2008. https://news.stanford.edu/news/2008/january16/wine-011608.html.

"According to a Norweigan study, over 20 million Americans have clinical-levels anxiety around flying." - "Flight Anxiety." Flight Safety Foundation, April 28, 2020.

https://flightsafety.org/asw-article/flight-anxiety/.

"After the terrorist attacks on September 11, 2001, Americans were less likely to travel by plane and prefered to go by car." - Blalock, Garrick, Vrinda Kadiyali, and Daniel H. Simon. "Driving Fatalities after 9/11: a Hidden Cost of Terrorism." *Applied Economics* 41, no. 14 (June 2009): 1717–29. https://doi.org/10.1080/00036840601069757.

"The reason we have these unrealistic expectations about air travel is because..." - Tversky, Amo, and Daniel Kahnema. "Availability: A Heuristic for Judging Frequency and Probability." *PsycEXTRA Dataset*, 1971. https://doi.org/10.1037/e301722005-001.

"One study of the top political pundits tracked all of the predictions they made about the future..." - Tetlock, Philip E. *Expert Political Judgment*, 2005.

"Numerous analyses of hedge fund data reveal that you would do just as well allowing a monkey to manage your portfolio than an MBA." - Ferri, Rick. "Any Monkey Can Beat The Market." Forbes. Forbes Magazine, December 15, 2020. https://www.forbes.com/sites/rickferri/2012/12/20/any-monkey-can-beat-the-market/.

"Another study of college admissions counselors investigated..." - Cashen, Valjean M. "Students', Parents', and Counselors' Prediction of Academic Success." *The Journal of Educational Research* 60, no. 5 (1967): 212-14. Accessed February 23, 2021. http://www.jstor.org/stable/27531848.

"Our self-concept is the most important schema we have." - Lieberman, Matthew D., Johanna M. Jarcho, and Ajay B. Satpute. "Evidence-Based and Intuition-Based Self-Knowledge: An FMRI Study." *Journal of Personality and Social Psychology* 87, no. 4 (2004): 421–35. https://doi.org/10.1037/0022-3514.87.4.421.

"This effect has been noted in a test regarding word memorization." - Jhangiani, Dr. Rajiv, Dr. Hammond Tarry, and Dr. Charles Stangor. "The Cognitive Self: The Self-Concept." Principles of Social Psychology 1st International Edition. BCcampus, September 26, 2014. https://opentextbc.ca/socialpsychology/chapter/the-cognitive-self-the-self-concept/.

"...we tend to take responsibility for desired outcomes while ignoring responsibility for undesirable outcomes." - Snyder, M. L., Stephan, W. G., & Rosenfield, D. (1976). Egotism and attribution. *Journal of Personality and Social Psychology, 33*(4), 435–441. https://doi.org/10.1037/0022-3514.33.4.435.

"However, we don't all have a high opinion of ourselves to protect." - Arkin, R. M., Appelman, A. J., & Burger, J. M. (1980). Social anxiety, self-presentation, and the self-serving bias in causal attribution. *Journal of Personality and Social Psychology, 38*(1), 23–35. https://doi.org/10.1037/0022-3514.38.1.23.

"In a study from Baumeister, Stillwell, and Wotman, the researchers analyzed participants' recounts of disputes." - Baumeister, Roy F., Arlene Stillwell, and Sara R. Wotman. "Victim and Perpetrator Accounts of Interpersonal Conflict: Autobiographical Narratives about Anger." *Journal of Personality and Social Psychology* 59, no. 5 (1990): 994–1005. https://doi.org/10.1037/0022-3514.59.5.994.

"Contesting who started the First World War is still up for debate." - "The Debate on the Origins of World War One." The British Library. The British Library, January 17, 2014. https://www.bl.uk/world-war-one/articles/the-debate-on-the-origins-of-world-war-one.

"Commonly, people reference self-sabotaging behaviors such as..." - Sappington, D.E.M., Weisman, D.L. Self-Sabotage. *J Regul Econ* 27, 155–175 (2005). https://doi.org/10.1007/s11149-004-5342-8.

"A study on athletes finds more instances of self-handicapping in individual sports than team sports." - Coudevylle, Guillaume R., Kathleen A. Ginis, Jean-Pierre Famose, and Christophe Gernigon. "Effects of Self-Handicapping Strategies on Anxiety before Athletic Performance." *The Sport Psychologist* 22, no. 3 (2008): 304–15. https://doi.org/10.1123/tsp.22.3.304.

"The most frequently cited real-life example of the bystander effect regards a young woman called Kitty Genovese..." - History.com Editors. "Kitty Genovese."

History.com. A&E Television Networks, January 5, 2018. https://www.history.com/topics/crime/kitty-genovese.

"In an experiment testing honesty, participants were asked to answer six quiz questions about music." - Hugh-Jones, David. (2015). Ways to measure honesty: a new experiment and two questionnaires.

"We don't like feeling inadequate, but we don't like disharmony either." - Festinger, L. (1957). *A theory of cognitive dissonance.* Stanford University Press.

"**According to self-awareness theory, when we focus our attention on ourselves…"** - Duval, S., & Wicklund, R. A. (1972). *A theory of objective self awareness.* Academic Press.

"No really, a study involving mirrors found that people felt significantly more distressed when…" - Phillips, Ann & Silvia, Paul. (2005). Self-Awareness and the Emotional Consequences of Self-Discrepancies. Personality & social psychology bulletin. 31. 703-13. 10.1177/0146167204271559.

"For example, Moskalenko and Heine found that people who are given false negative feedback…" - Moskalenko, Sophia & Heine, Steven. (2003). Watching Your Troubles Away: Television Viewing as a Stimulus for Subjective Self-Awareness. Personality & social psychology bulletin. 29. 76-85. 10.1177/0146167202238373.

"Munro and Stansbury made a study of attacking participants' self-concepts." - Munro, Geoffrey & Stansbury, Jessica. (2009). The Dark Side of Self-Affirmation: Confirmation Bias and Illusory Correlation in Response to Threatening Information. Personality & social psychology bulletin. 35. 1143-53. 10.1177/0146167209337163.

"The psychological term for maintaining a position despite contradictory evidence is self-deception." - Deweese-Boyd, Ian. "Self-Deception." Stanford Encyclopedia of Philosophy. Stanford University, November 7, 2016. https://plato.stanford.edu/entries/self-deception/.

"The more we lie to ourselves, the more wrapped up we become in our illusion and it can even influence our memories." - Mitchell, Terence R., Leigh Thompson, Erika Peterson, and Randy Cronk. "Temporal Adjustments in the Evaluation of Events: The 'Rosy View.'" *Journal of Experimental Social Psychology* 33, no. 4 (1997): 421–48. https://doi.org/10.1006/jesp.1997.1333.

"Psychologists have discovered that human memory doesn't work like a movie." - Exton-McGuinness, Marc T.J., Jonathan L.C. Lee, and Amy C. Reichelt. "Updating Memories—The Role of Prediction Errors in Memory Reconsolidation." *Behavioural Brain Research* 278 (2015): 375–84. https://doi.org/10.1016/j.bbr.2014.10.011.

"In psychological experiments, researchers have successfully inserted false events into participants' childhood memories." - Brewin, Chris R., and Bernice Andrews. "Creating Memories for False Autobiographical Events in Childhood: A Systematic Review." *Applied Cognitive Psychology* 31, no. 1 (2016): 2–23. https://doi.org/10.1002/acp.3220.

"A similar test demonstrated how these types of suggestions can magically turn yield signs into stop signs…" - Zaragoza, Maria & Belli, Robert & Payment, Kristie. (2007). Misinformation Effects and the Suggestibility of Eyewitness Memory.

"In a study at a horse race, experimenters asked people waiting in the two-dollar-bet line…" - Slovic, Paul, and Amos Tversky. "Who Accepts Savage's Axiom?" *PsycEXTRA Dataset*, 1974. https://doi.org/10.1037/e457842004-001.

"Another entertaining place to observe high-stakes self-deception is in the BigFoot hunting community." - MINNESOTA BIGFOOT RESEARCH TEAM. Accessed February 23, 2021. http://mnbrt.com/index.html.

"I know a website that features organic wellness oils alongside concoctions designed to attract BigFoot." - Price, Mark. "NC Mom Invents a Spray She Says Will Attract Any Bigfoot within a Mile and a Half." The Charlotte Observer, September 13, 2013. https://www.charlotteobserver.com/news/local/article173012526.html.

"Instead, after the crash, they offered Holly's bandmates, the Crickets, extra money to complete the tour without Holly." - Chronicle, The Muskegon. "Letters: Remembering Buddy Holly on Valentine's Day." mlive, February 14, 2011. https://www.mlive.com/opinion/muskegon/2011/02/letters_remembering_buddy_holl.html.

"The Victim's Rights policy was subsequently adopted..." - Jamie Osborne September 14, 2020. "How the Tragic Death of Buddy Holly Led to a Crucial Government Law Change." Far Out Magazine. Accessed February 23, 2021. https://faroutmagazine.co.uk/buddy-holly-death-law-change/.

Chapter 2

"One of the most notable studies on disillusionment happened in the winter of 1955..." - Festinger, Leon, Stanley Schacter, and Henry W. Riecken. *When Prophecy Fails: by Leon Festinger, Henry W. Riecken and Stanley Schacter*. Minneapolis: University of Minnesota Press, 1956.

"They say a bird in the hand is worth two in the bush..." - Shaikh, Amreen Bashir. "Proverb Origins – A Bird in the Hand Is Worth Two in the Bush." aka The Versatile, September 3, 2015. https://akatheversatile.com/2015/09/05/proverb-origins-a-bird-in-the-hand-is-worth-two-in-the-bush/.

"Some studies have found this effect trickling all the way down to a single nickel." - Homonoff, Tatiana A. "Can Small Incentives Have Large Effects? The Impact of Taxes versus Bonuses on Disposable Bag Use." *American Economic Journal: Economic Policy* 10, no. 4 (2018): 177–210. https://doi.org/10.1257/pol.20150261.

"In a study from 1991, participants were given a mug and then offered the chance to sell it..." - Kahneman, Daniel, Jack L. Knetsch, and Richard H. Thaler. "Anomalies: The Endowment Effect, Loss Aversion, and Status Quo Bias." *Choices, Values, and Frames*, 2000, 159–70. https://doi.org/10.1017/cbo9780511803475.009.

"In 1984, Knetsch and Sinden demonstrated this effect with unmistakable accuracy." - Knetsch, Jack L., and J. A. Sinden. "Willingness to Pay and Compensation Demanded: Experimental Evidence of an Unexpected Disparity in Measures of Value." *The Quarterly Journal of Economics* 99, no. 3 (1984): 507. https://doi.org/10.2307/1885962.

"Further research has demonstrated that we will accept larger risks to avoid losses..." - Schindler, S., & Pfattheicher, S. (2017). The frame of the game: Loss-framing increases dishonest behavior. *Journal of Experimental Social Psychology, 69*, 172–177. https://doi.org/10.1016/j.jesp.2016.09.009.

"In one study, people were tasked with completing anagrams and they were rewarded in two different ways." - Grolleau, Gilles, Martin G. Kocher, and Angela Sutan. "Cheating and Loss Aversion: Do People Cheat More to Avoid a Loss?" *Management Science* 62, no. 12 (2016): 3428–38. https://doi.org/10.1287/mnsc.2015.2313.

"In another study, researchers hypothesized that people with higher stakes might be more likely to quit an unhealthy habit." - Halpern, Scott D., Benjamin French, Dylan S. Small, Kathryn Saulsgiver, Michael O. Harhay, Janet Audrain-McGovern, George Loewenstein, Troyen A. Brennan, David A. Asch, and Kevin G. Volpp. "Randomized Trial of Four Financial-Incentive Programs for Smoking Cessation." *New England Journal of Medicine* 372, no. 22 (2015): 2108–17. https://doi.org/10.1056/nejmoa1414293.

"In 1995, the American Psychological Association was fascinated by the 1992 Summer Olympics held in Barcelona, Spain." - Medvec, Victoria & Madey, Scott & Gilovich, Thomas. (1995). When Less Is More: Counterfactual Thinking and Satisfaction Among Olympic Medalists. Journal of personality and social psychology. 69. 603-10. 10.1037/0022-3514.69.4.603.

"Humans attach more meaning to bad experiences." - Baumeister, Roy F., Ellen Bratslavsky, Catrin Finkenauer, and Kathleen D. Vohs. "Bad Is Stronger than Good." *Review of General Psychology* 5, no. 4 (2001): 323–70. https://doi.org/10.1037//1089-2680.5.4.323.

"Studies have suggested that negativity bias shows up in babies at as early as seven months of age." - Grossmann, Tobias, Tricia Striano, and Angela D. Friederici. "Developmental Changes in Infants' Processing of Happy and Angry Facial Expressions: A Neurobehavioral Study." *Brain and Cognition* 64, no. 1 (2007): 30–41. https://doi.org/10.1016/j.bandc.2006.10.002.

"Research has demonstrated that performance under pressure is modulated by our confidence that we have everything under control." - Otten, Mark. "Choking vs. Clutch Performance: A Study of Sport Performance under Pressure." *Journal of Sport and Exercise Psychology* 31, no. 5 (2009): 583–601. https://doi.org/10.1123/jsep.31.5.583.

"The Pygmalion effect demonstrates how expectations from teachers can improve or fetter students' performances." - Rosenthal, Robert, and Lenore Jacobson. "Pygmalion in the Classroom." *The Urban Review* 3, no. 1 (1968): 16–20. https://doi.org/10.1007/bf02322211.

"One way to demonstrate the confusion between a successful outcome and a successful process is through the clustering illusion." - Kahneman, Daniel, and Amos Tversky. "Subjective Probability: A Judgment of Representativeness." *Cognitive Psychology* 3, no. 3 (1972): 430–54. https://doi.org/10.1016/0010-0285(72)90016-3.

"A look at stock portfolios finds that traders who experienced the greatest losses were the ones who experienced early successes." - Walk, The Rational. "The Pitfalls of Early Success – A Personal History: The Rational Walk." The Rational Walk |, August 13, 2020. https://rationalwalk.com/the-pitfalls-of-early-success-a-personal-history/.

"These examples of the clustering illusion feed into a greater bias known as confirmation bias." - Nickerson, Raymond S. "Confirmation Bias: A Ubiquitous Phenomenon in Many Guises." *Review of General Psychology* 2, no. 2 (1998): 175–220. https://doi.org/10.1037/1089-2680.2.2.175.

"We can see the power expectations have on perception if we look at the McGurk effect." - McGurk, H., & MacDonald, J. (1976). Hearing lips and seeing voices. *Nature, 264*(5588), 746–748. https://doi.org/10.1038/264746a0.

"The most curious thing about the McGurk effect is that being aware of it does not save you from it." - "McGurk Effect - Auditory Illusion - BBC Horizon Clip - YouTube." Accessed February 23, 2021. https://www.youtube.com/watch?v=2k8fHR9jKVM.

"There's a story behind the Chinese idiom "lan yu chong shu" that speaks to the effects of an ongoing illusion." - Lvli. "Chinese Idiom Lan YU Chong Shu - China: Mandarin." HSK, September 5, 2020. https://www.chinesehsk.com/hsk/chinese-idiom-lan-yu-chong-shu/.

"It's the opposite of a better known effect called guilty by association..." - "Examples of Guilt by Association." Example Articles & Resources. Accessed February 23, 2021. https://examples.yourdictionary.com/examples-of-guilt-by-association.html.

"The movie *The Room* is wildly famous because Tommy Wiseau over-valued his own story, acting, and directing skills." - Romano, Aja. "The Room: How the Worst Movie Ever Became a Hollywood Legend as Bizarre as Its Creator." Vox. Vox, December 2, 2017. https://www.vox.com/culture/2017/12/2/16720012/the-room-tommy-wiseau-backstory-explained.

"*The Disaster Artist* made 1.2 million dollars on opening day." - "The Disaster Artist." Box Office Mojo. Accessed February 23, 2021. https://www.boxofficemojo.com/release/rl1979942401/.

Chapter 3

"Cognitive psychologist Daniel Gilbert calls the brain an 'anticipation machine.'" - Gilbert, Daniel Todd. *Stumbling on Happiness*. New York: Vintage, 2007.

"Studies show that about 77 percent of us keep our New Year's resolutions past the first week..." - Norcross, John & Vangarelli, Dominic. (1988). The resolution solution: Longitudinal examination of New Year's change attempts. Journal of Substance Abuse. 1. 127-134. 10.1016/S0899-3289(88)80016-6.

"Among Americans who are making New Year's resolutions, an online survey reveals..." - "US_New_Years_Resolutions_2020.Xlsx," n.d. URL: https://docs.cdn.yougov.com/2v6sawx0rr/US_New_Years_Resolutions_2020.pdf

"Motivation can be internal or external." - Ryan, Richard M., and Edward L. Deci. "Intrinsic and Extrinsic Motivations: Classic Definitions and New Directions." *Contemporary Educational Psychology* 25, no. 1 (2000): 54–67. https://doi.org/10.1006/ceps.1999.1020.

"In fact, the best-known model for creativity and innovation in the workplace by Amabile (1988)..." - Amabile, Teresa M. "A Model of Creativity and Innovation in Organizations." Essay. In *Research in Organizational Behavior* 10, 10:123–67. JAI Press Inc., 1988.

"A 1988 study demonstrates that children who were rewarded for playing with a toy..." - Fabes, R.A., Eisenberg, N., Fultz, J. *et al.* Reward, affect, and young children's motivational orientation. *Motiv Emot* 12, 155–169 (1988). https://doi.org/10.1007/BF00992171.

"In 1906, a monumental, but now antiquated, ethnographic survey from Finnish philosopher Edvard Westermarck identified..." - Ellis, H. (1906). The Origin and Development of the Moral Ideas, By Edward Westermarck, Ph.D. Vol. 1. London: Macmillan. 1906. Pp. 716, 8vo. Price 14s. *Journal of Mental Science*, *52*(218), 589-591. doi:10.1192/bjp.52.218.589.

"Moral studies from O'Neill & Petrinovich (1998), Henrich et al. (2005), and Hauser,et al. (2007) converge on two commonalities that persist throughout all humanity..."

- O'Neill, P., & Petrinovich, L. (1998). A preliminary cross-cultural study of moral intuitions. *Evolution and Human Behavior, 19*(6), 349–367. https://doi.org/10.1016/S1090-5138(98)00030-0.

- Henrich, Joseph, Robert Boyd, Samuel Bowles, Colin Camerer, Ernst Fehr, Herbert Gintis, Richard McElreath, et al. "'Economic Man' in Cross-Cultural Perspective: Behavioral Experiments in 15 Small-Scale Societies." *Behavioral and Brain Sciences* 28, no. 6 (2005): 795–815. https://doi.org/10.1017/s0140525x05000142.

- Hauser, Marc & CUSHMAN, FIERY & YOUNG, LIANE & Jin, R. & MIKHAIL, JOHN. (2007). A Dissociation Between Moral Judgments and Justification. Mind & Language - MIND LANG. 22. 1-21. 10.1111/j.1468-0017.2006.00297.x.

"In 1957, Leon Festinger devised the most boring task imaginable to test cognitive dissonance theory..." - Festinger, Leon, and James M. Carlsmith. "Cognitive Consequences of Forced Compliance." *The Journal of Abnormal and Social Psychology* 58, no. 2 (1959): 203–10. https://doi.org/10.1037/h0041593.

Chapter 4

"The election of 1861 would decide who would bear the onus of leading America through a civil war." - Goodwin, Doris Kearns. *Team of Rivals: the Political Genius of Abraham Lincoln*. London: Penguin, 2013.

"In this wood engraving from Frank Leslie's Illustrated Newspaper, February 2, 1861..." - A Job for the New Cabinet Maker. , 1861. Photograph. https://www.loc.gov/item/2006684372/.

"**This simple test demonstrates how we can have blindspots that we aren't aware of until we put them to the test.**" - Gamm, D. M. and Albert, . Daniel M.. "Blind spot." Encyclopedia Britannica, January 31, 2020. https://www.britannica.com/science/blind-spot.

"**Imagine you are asked to watch a short video in which six people pass basketballs around.**" - The Invisible Gorilla: And Other Ways Our Intuitions Deceive Us. Accessed February 23, 2021. http://www.theinvisiblegorilla.com/gorilla_experiment.html.

"**While his secretaries initially resented Lincoln for his success, they grew to respect his decision-making skills.**" - Chervinsky, Lindsay M. "Abraham Lincoln's Cabinet." WHHA (en-US), May 29, 2020. https://www.whitehousehistory.org/abraham-lincolns-cabinet.

"**Judas was one of the Twelve Apostles of Jesus Christ...**" - Matthew 26:14-15 (New International Version)

"**Judas led religious authorities to Jesus while he was alone praying in a field and gave him the infamous 'Judas Kiss' to identify him to the captors.**" - Matthew 26:47-56, Mark 14:43 (Holman Christian Standard Bible)

"**This famous line of betrayal comes from William Shakespeare's *Julius Caesar*...**" - Shakespeare, William. "Julius Caesar." 1599.

"**The Manhattan Project gathered some of the greatest scientific minds in the world to create an atomic bomb...**" - "Spies Who Spilled Atomic Bomb Secrets." Smithsonian.com. Smithsonian Institution, April 19, 2009. https://www.smithsonianmag.com/history/spies-who-spilled-atomic-bomb-secrets-127922660/.

"**This was likely the case with Justin Beiber's team, who didn't feel secure enough to tell Justin about one of his embarrassing blindspots.**" - "Justin Bieber Wardrobe Malfunction: Fly Down At Concert." The BBS 2.0, March 14, 2011. https://thebieberspace.wordpress.com/2011/03/13/305/.

"**The Light Triad is a group of personality traits that are commonly found in the world's most well-reputable people.**" - Kaufman, Scott Barry. "The Light Triad vs. Dark Triad of Personality." Scientific American Blog Network. Scientific American, March 19, 2019. https://blogs.scientificamerican.com/beautiful-minds/the-light-triad-vs-dark-triad-of-personality/.

"**In November 2019, Mina Chang resigned from her senior State Department post...**" - Luce, Dan De, Laura Strickler, and Ari Sen. "How Did Mina Chang Get a State Department Job in the First Place?" NBCNews.com. NBCUniversal News Group, November 27, 2019. https://www.nbcnews.com/politics/donald-trump/how-did-mina-chang-get-state-department-job-first-place-n1091516.

"**In another case from 2018, dozens had been charged in an admissions fraud scandal...**" - Medina, Jennifer, Katie Benner, and Kate Taylor. "Actresses, Business Leaders and Other Wealthy Parents Charged in U.S. College Entry Fraud." The New York Times. The New York Times, March 12, 2019. https://www.nytimes.com/2019/03/12/us/college-admissions-cheating-scandal.html.

"**Take Power Balance for example. In their advertising...**" - Diaz, Jesus. "PowerBalance Admits Their Wristbands Are a Scam." Gizmodo. Gizmodo, June 18, 2013. https://gizmodo.com/powerbalance-admits-their-wristbands-are-a-scam-5723577.

"**Physician Andrew Wakefield came from a background of successful doctors.**" - Omer, Saad B. "The Discredited Doctor Hailed by the Anti-Vaccine Movement." Nature News. Nature Publishing Group, October 27, 2020. https://www.nature.com/articles/d41586-020-02989-9.

"**...in 1993 when he published reports of the measles virus causing Crohn's disease, which was later disproved.**" - Wakefield, A. J., R. M. Pittilo, R. Sim, S. L. Cosby, J. R. Stephenson, A. P. Dhillon, and R. E. Pounder. "Evidence of Persistent Measles Virus Infection in Crohn's Disease." *Journal of Medical Virology* 39, no. 4 (1993): 345–53. https://doi.

org/10.1002/jmv.1890390415.

   "In a 2010 investigation, the public learned that Wakefield and his colleagues had altered facts about the children in their study."
-   Ross, Oakland. "Andrew Wakefield's Fraudulent Vaccine Research." thestar.com, January 7, 2011. https://www.thestar.com/news/insight/article/918362--andrew-wakefield-s-fraudulent-research.
-   British doctor resigns as head of Austin autism center. Accessed February 23, 2021. https://web.archive.org/web/20100312134206/http://www.statesman.com/news/local/british-doctor-resigns-as-head-of-austin-autism-251756.html.

   "Google Ventures partner Jake Knapp finds that interviewing five people exposes 85% of the problems with a new product." - Knapp, Jake, John Zeratsky, and Braden Kowitz. *Sprint: How to Solve Big Problems and Test New Ideas in Just Five Days*. New York: Simon & Schuster, 2016.

   "In hunter-gatherer days human tribes rarely exceeded 150 people..." - "Dunbar's Number: Why We Can Only Maintain 150 Relationships." BBC Future. BBC. Accessed February 23, 2021. https://www.bbc.com/future/article/20191001-dunbars-number-why-we-can-only-maintain-150-relationships.

   "The example of the Battle of Cannae illustrates this." - Daly, Gregory. *Cannae: the Experience of Battle in the Second Punic War*. London: Routledge, 2004.

Chapter 5

   "In 2010, three Belgian skydivers found themselves in a high-stakes love triangle." - "Belgian Skydiver 'Murdered Love Rival' during Jump." BBC News. BBC, September 24, 2010. https://www.bbc.com/news/world-europe-11404581.

   "There's an unsettling Wikipedia page that documents over 200 hazing-related deaths in American fraternities." - "List of Hazing Deaths in the United States." Wikipedia. Wikimedia Foundation, February 20, 2021. https://en.wikipedia.org/wiki/List_of_hazing_deaths_in_the_United_States.

   "On November 3rd, 1948, the *Chicago Tribune* incorrectly declared New York Governor Thomas Dewey the next U.S. President..." - "Newspaper Mistakenly Declares 'Dewey Defeats Truman.'" History.com. A&E Television Networks, November 16, 2009. https://www.history.com/this-day-in-history/newspaper-mistakenly-declares-dewey-president.

   "In the 90s, scientists such as Jackson, Koek, and Colpaert put rats into mazes..." - Jackson, A., Koek, W., & Colpaert, F. C. (1992). NMDA antagonists make learning and recall state-dependent. *Behavioural pharmacology*, *3*(4), 415–421. https://doi.org/10.1097/00008877-199208000-00018.

   "Bilingual people are able to recall more information when tested in the same language they used to learn the material." - Marian, V., Kaushanskaya, M. Language context guides memory content. *Psychonomic Bulletin & Review* 14, 925–933 (2007). https://doi.org/10.3758/BF03194123.

   "Godden and Baddeley demonstrate that context matters too. In 1975..." - Koens, F., Ten Cate, O. T., & Custers, E. J. (2003). Context-dependent memory in a meaningful environment for medical education: in the classroom and at the bedside. *Advances in health sciences education : theory and practice*, *8*(2), 155–165. https://doi.org/10.1023/a:1024993619713.

   "Further, it is easier to recall unpleasant memories than pleasant ones when we're sad, and easier to recall pleasant memories than unpleasant ones when we're happy."
-   Bower, G. H. (1981). Mood and memory. *American Psychologist*, *36*(2), 129–148. https://doi.org/10.1037/0003-066X.36.2.129.

- Eich, Darin. "A Grounded Theory of High-Quality Leadership Programs." *Journal of Leadership & Organizational Studies* 15, no. 2 (2008): 176–87. https://doi.org/10.1177/1548051808324099.

"Long term potentiation (LTP) adds fuel to the fire. LTP is the strengthening..." - Hall, Richard H. "Long Term Potentiation," 1998. https://web.mst.edu/~rhall/neuroscience/05_simple_learning/ltp.pdf.

Acknowledgements

I want to thank all the people in my life who made a difference. Most are alive, fortunately. Some have deceased. These names are in alphabetical order. I also want to give a special thanks to my children, as they are my heroes, and my friend Kevin Walter who has helped me assemble and organize this book.

Abraham D. Lancry, Alfonso Vason, Andy Kabot, Angela M. Lancry, Anthony Oborny, Arash Tirgan, Armond Waxman, Barry Lampl, Bernie Kosar, Brian Jacobson, Brock Milstein, Charles Schnieber, Chuck Camble, Dave Walter, Dick Bass, Gary Catania, Gary Russo, Gayle Waxman, Gregg Waxman, Jamie Pilla, Jay and Tabitha Luzar, Jillian Swaninger, John Bowers, Jonathan Leebow, Katelyn N. Lancry, Lindsey Hutchinson, Marc Jacobson, Mark Lyon, Michael Hennenburg, Michael Mihalic, Neil Cornrich, Norm Hamilton, Rich Koblentz, Stephanie LeBlond, Todd Waxman, my grandmother and grandfather, and my other dear friends and family members as there are too many names to mention. May life continue to bless you now and always as you have blessed mine.

Love,
Nathan